Masonic Regularity and Recognition

MASONIC REGULARITY
and
RECOGNITION

A Global Issue

Roger Dachez

With a foreword by
Alain Bauer

Westphalia Press
An Imprint of the Policy Studies Organization
Washington, DC
2016

Westphalia Press
An imprint of Policy Studies Organization
1527 New Hampshire Ave., NW
Washington, D.C. 20036
info@ipsonet.org

ISBN-10: 1-63391-384-8
ISBN-13: 978-1-63391-384-4

Cover and interior design by Jeffrey Barnes
jbarnesbook.design

Daniel Gutierrez-Sandoval, Executive Director
PSO and Westphalia Press

Updated material and comments on this edition
can be found at the Westphalia Press website:
www.westphaliapress.org

CONTENTS

FOREWORD
IN SEARCH OF LOST REGULARITY?

In 1999, as a young counselor to the Order of the Grand Orient de France (GODF), I found myself discovering the charms of Masonic diplomacy. There were difficult internal relations after a convent that had seen the 'GO' close to explosion, complicated dialogue with what was then the Grand Collège des Rites (Grand College of the Rites), and a very disturbed international situation with the crisis of CLIPSAS.

And above all, in the middle of everything and as an immediate subject of dialogue between Brothers, there was a sort of reduction *ad regularitam*, which dominated any discussion within minutes.

This inspired me to research regularity, and I published a short work, 'De la régularité' (On Regularity), some parts of which are used here.

As Roger Dachez, my friend and Brother, reminds us here with his characteristic learnedness and a clear touch of frustration, the more we look, the more the supposed evidence seems to evade us, just as the horizon flees an explorer.

Etymologically and historically speaking, a *règle*—French for 'rule', from the Latin *regula* (principle)—is:

- A long, straight instrument used to draw straight lines.
- That which serves to direct, lead, or rule.
- An example or a model.

- The constitution of a religious order.

Regularity (or, in French, *régularité*) is therefore that which is regular, harmony and the observation of duties.

- What is a regular [régulier] Mason? A Mason who is a member of a regular Lodge.
- What is a regular Lodge? A Lodge that has constitutions accorded or renewed by the Grand Orient de France, which alone has the right to give them.

In 1773, these words laid out the substance of articles II and III of the first constitution of the Grand Orient de France.

English Freemasons approached the problem differently. During a quarrel that began in 1751, one of the Grand Lodges called itself the Lodge of the 'Most Antient [oldest] and Honourable Fraternity of Free and Accepted Masons of England'. Regularity is not the issue here: just age and this evocation of acceptance, or rather recognition, approval.

Here lies the essence of our debate. It is based only on diplomatic data and therefore on political relations between Obediences. Until the 1950s, the *Grand Orient de France* continued unwaveringly granting diplomas for Masters or patents for Lodges, saluting 'regular' Freemasons around the world. However, insidiously, doubt was growing. Only the departure of SHAPE (NATO's integrated headquarters) finally triggered a real break with most American Grand Lodges. The moderate and then faster expansion of a division of the Grand Orient de France (the GLNF), which took almost 40 years to take into account the 1877 vote before leaving, and the failure of the rapprochement with the Grande Loge de France in

1945 created the conditions for serious doubt within the Grand Orient de France. This initially relative issue began to nag, and then developed into a real obsession. The word 'regularity' (*régularité*) itself came to be used only with infinite care. Official references to it ceased. It was no longer used in diplomas and patents. This was less a challenge or the assertion of a new freedom than a doubt or, perhaps, even a vague kind of shame.

Yet Anderson specified in General Head I of the *Charges* that:

> A Mason is *oblig'd* by his Tenure, to obey the moral Law; and if he rightly understands the Art, he will never be a stupid Atheist, nor an irreligious Libertine. But though in ancient Times Masons were charg'd in every Country to be of the Religion of that Country or Nation, whatever it was, yet 'tis now thought more expedient only to oblige them to that Religion in which all Men agree, leaving their particular Opinions to themselves; that is, to be good Men and true, or Men of Honour and Honesty, by whatever Denominations or Persuasions they may be distinguish'd; whereby Masonry becomes the Center of Union, and the *M*eans of conciliating true *F*riendship among *P*ersons that must else have remain'd at a perpetual Distance.

Often, newcomers tried to convince others that they were established in order to obtain recognition and regularity, with no qualms about confusing the two. Having lived in the United States and having been received, ex officio, into a 'regular' Lodge, I am familiar with the subtleties and the flexibility of recognition among Brothers in the United States (and sometimes in England). Many people would be surprised by the quality of the dialogue maintained between London, New York or California and Paris during these recent crises. And this dialogue most often took place through the wise and enlightened Roger Dachez and a group of peacekeepers in Freemasonry, who wanted diversity in Masonic careers in accordance with different identities.

Roger Dachez is undoubtedly the most 'regular' among us, due to his work, the recognition of his qualities throughout the Masonic world and his opposition to lies and compromises of principles.

The Americans, English, French and many others do not all see regularity in the same way. To them, it is as much a qualitative tool (You understand the shared rules) as a political measure (The territory allows us to construct the Obedience that bestows the titles.) This is comparable to how the way we learn to drive allows the existence of good drivers without a license and bad drivers with one.

Subtly, American Masons have used a flexible approach. They have let London decide upon the hard assertion of the Dogma, preferring to use their moral viewpoint as a tool for dialogue, with California at the forefront.[1] This makes it possible to meet, talk about history and culture, and obtain a lot by demanding nothing. However, if people lie to them, often brazenly in order to obtain something, they are sent to carry out in-depth study. The Paris International Conference on the Brotherhood has successfully strengthened this process since 2015.

---

[1] Albert Pike's excellent *Morals and Dogma* can never be read too many times.

This book is therefore part of the journey made by those who search for truth through the practice of virtue.

By those who recognise themselves as such.

Because initiation has made them Sisters and Brothers and because the regulation of chaos, as Jean Mourgues might have put it, obviously needs obedience, rules and recognition.

However, as with states, it is possible not to recognise the government while accepting that the country does exist.

Alain Bauer
Freemason

Preface

This little book is the result of a piercing frustration: my own, over the last two years (2012–2014), in the face of the artificial positions and pretenses that have peppered the Masonic landscape in France, since what later historical writings might refer to as the 'Call of Basel' (June 2012). Following the 'de-recognition' of the Grande Loge Nationale Française (GLNF) in 2012, the Grande Loge de France (GLDF) wanted to take its place as the 'regular' obedience in France. We know that this effort, which was both unreasonable and poorly prepared, was a complete failure.

However, above all, at this time in France, various parties had adopted tactical positions that were sometimes difficult to understand and to maintain. They had used confusingly ambiguous discourse, or to support their cause, they had called upon 'experts', using doublespeak or disguising the facts, more out of professional strategy than to honestly enlighten Masonic opinion.

This led to distressing disorder, which did nothing to improve the image of French Freemasonry. Even if we forget the unbelievably aggressive insults and invectives that flourished in forums and on blogs, which tell us much about what Freemasonry means for those who wrote them, this regrettable episode was merely another expression of the worrying incoherence of the French Masonic landscape. I am not referring here to its diversity, which is an unavoidable and definitive fact of its history, but to that which is supposed to give all French Freemasons a shared identity, in spite of everything.

The label 'regularity' has been at the centre of debates and brought out divides that go far beyond the expected[2] shipwreck of an issue that was poorly constructed from the start. The Call of Basel revealed a vision and a practice of Masonry that have been prevalent in France for well over a century, and have condemned it to regular upheavals and disputes. These are rather ridiculous in that they are generally based on a worrying lack of understanding of the basics of Masonic tradition, vagaries in the history of Freemasonry and, above all, a profound ignorance about what Freemasonry really is around the world, for the vast majority of Masons.

This unlikely vaudeville that has been the chronicle of French Masonry over the last few decades, a collection of warlike declarations and slammed doors, with under inspired or poorly inspired—and above all misinformed—dignitaries missing many chances to keep their mouths shut, is in fact the expression of a more fundamental and therefore more serious problem, but also a more interesting one.

The events of the 2012–2014 tragicomedy (of which the only tangible result was to make the French Masonic

---

[2] Particularly by M. Barat, A. Bauer, and me from September 2013 in *Les Promesses de l'aube*, and in August 2013 on my blog, from which the following passage is taken: 'People use words without knowing what they mean, they talk about the *Basic Principles* but misunderstand their nature, and above all, they talk about regularity without comprehending what it means, let alone what it implies. In this context, how can we be surprised when chaos and cacophony ensue, against a background of bitterness and aggressive attitudes?' (Roger Dachez, 'Les Promesses de l'aube': un pamphlet?', *Pierres Vivantes* (blog), August 28, 2013, http://pierresvivantes. hautetfort.com/archive/2013/08/28/temp-52c8b50124dfed-a9e03e76f0852ec258-5150625.html).

landscape even more complicated and stir up many long-term grudges) undoubtedly brought the highly unusual nature of the French Masonic model in the world back to the surface. This in itself is not necessarily a problem. The real issue is above all the heavily French focus of a Masonry that, 'regular' or otherwise, has a strong tendency to see its choices as absolute, to reduce the whole Masonic institution to its own specific identity and, to top it all, to hold this up as a universal norm!

I hope that this brief study can find its place at the crossroads of this current state that must be escaped, these contradictions that must be untangled and this blindness that must be cured.

My aim in writing was to be sincere and without hidden intentions, and I cannot be reproached for ever saying the opposite of what I think or doing the opposite of what I say. I have also been careful to state my sources and references, but I do not claim to be infallible, and I offer my work as an honest contribution that is nevertheless naturally open to criticism, and to a problematic debate.

However, my aim is not to deceive my readers, or to deliberately or spinelessly sweeten the pill, or to lead them down dead ends. My Masonic choices are known and do not interfere here, because I do not take sides. Personally, philosophically, and morally, I adhere to a traditional and 'regular' view of Freemasonry, but I do not belong to a Grand Lodge that is 'recognised' by the globally predominant Masonic community.[3] This choice, which is my private business, does not influence my work: it is time that distance from the subject of study became the norm

---

[3] I am a member of a very small Obedience, the Loge Nationale Française (LNF), created in 1968 from the GLNF. Its motto is 'God is our Guide.'

for debate in the French Masonic world, just as it is in the academic circles where Freemasonry once recruited its members.

For my own part, I strive, in contrast to some all-too-well-known 'leading historians', to live by my truth, even if it is debatable, rather than by concealed and always contemptible lies.

Finally, by having this work translated into English, I want to give American and British Freemasons a sincere and genuine representation of French Masonry, which is such a complex landscape that even the French themselves sometimes become lost in it. I also hope to definitively overcome the half lies and ambivalences that have led French Obediences to give the American Masonic authorities a partly falsified representation.

The issue of regularity and recognition in Freemasonry is examined here from a mainly French point of view, because France is essentially the only major Masonic country in the world where this debate is so complicated. However, in working to re-address the matter from this specific angle, I also think that it is possible to bring out questions that go well beyond the purely French context and that might be useful for a truly global approach to the problem.

I want to believe in and fervently wish for the rise of a global Masonic community that is reconciled with itself. However, this can only happen against a background of transparency and intellectual honesty. This, I hope, will be the contribution of this modest study.

CHAPTER 1
EVERYONE'S REGULAR!

What great times we live in—at least in the French Masonic world, where everyone is 'regular'!

This is the unusual and pleasing consequence of the entirely uncontrolled and above all unthinking use of a word that acts as a sort of talisman and that everyone lays claim to and adopts shamelessly, without really worrying about where it comes from, or what it meant when it was introduced into Masonic language.

First of all, there are 'official' (if I dare use the word) regulars who claim Anglo-Saxon regularity—a subject that I will examine in more detail later. Undeniably, they have the privilege of being the largest Masonic community in the world. If we estimate, with a reasonable margin of error of 10%, that there are around 2.5 million Masons[4] in the world, 'Anglo-Saxon regular' Masonry accounts for around 90% of the total. In other words, around 90% of all Freemasons in the world call themselves 'regular' and share this description. In substance, the definition that they give to it is expressed by a few very similar and on the whole non-contradictory fundamental texts. These include the *Basic Principles for Recognition* by the United Grand Lodge of England (UGLE), adopted on September 4, 1929, and the *Aims and Relationships of the Craft*, a declaration shared by the three Home Grand Lodges

---

[4] With around 1.3 million in the United States, three hundred thousand in England, and fewer than one hundred thousand for the whole of Scotland and Ireland. Global figures of four or five million, still cited by some, correspond to the situation in the 1960s and 1970s, and not at all to the current situation.

(England, Scotland, and Ireland) that dates back to August 4, 1949.[5] We can also add a much shorter and under cited text that is very important in the United States, namely the *Standards of Recognition* set down in 1952 by the Commission on Information for Recognition, before the Conference of Grand Masters in North America—the COGMINA (United States, Canada and Mexico).[6]

If we stick to the major principles, which we can describe as 'more sensitive' than the others, we are left with five, from the most to the least important:[7]

- The belief in a 'Great Architect of the Universe and His revealed will' (England 1929), or even more clearly in 'God' (United States 1952), a requirement that 'admits of no compromise' (Home Grand Lodges 1949). The Volume of Sacred Law, an essential element of the Lodge (England 1929, United States 1952), signifying 'the revelation from above' (England 1929), thus gives 'a sacred character' to the initiate's vow (Home Grand Lodges 1949).

- A ban on political and religious debates (England 1929, Home Grand Lodges 1949, United States 1952).

- A ban on inter-visiting with members of 'irregular' Masonic bodies, in particular including those with female members (England 1929,

---

[5] In fact, discussions began in 1938. It was solemnly reaffirmed in 2009.

[6] The three texts are reproduced in full in the appendices of this book.

[7] This is my classification, and it is therefore debatable, but it seems to me to be quite well aligned with the general feeling in Anglo-Saxon Masonic circles.

Home Grand Lodges 1949).

- The independence of Symbolic Lodges regarding the jurisdictions of the high degrees (England 1929, Home Grand Lodges 1949).
- Regularity of origin (England 1929, United States 1952).

However, in France, many other Masons believe and claim that they are 'regular.'

The Grand Orient de France (GODF), which long ostensibly neglected this quality, re-introduced it into its official headers from 2002. These now read: 'Grand Orient de France—Sovereign Regular Symbolic Power' (before this date, it was only 'symbolic and sovereign'.) however, it is perfectly clear that the largest and the oldest French Masonic obedience (which is 'liberal' and 'humanist', and has more recently begun calling itself 'adogmatic', and is, moreover, for both men and women!) is to say the least rather distant from Anglo-Saxon Masonry, particularly when it comes to the issues of belief in a Supreme Being and 'societal' debates.

For its part, the Grande Loge de France (GLDF), founded in 1894 in its current form, has never followed the letter of the *Basic Principles*. In particular, it has always openly admitted agnostics and atheists[8] and left the 'symbol' of the Great Architect of the Universe open to interpretation by its members. Moreover, these fundamental texts do not forbid speeches and debates on matters of so-

---

[8] GLDF website: '*Your questions.* 7. Must a person believe in God to be a Freemason in the Grande Loge de France? No, unlike Obediences that demand belief in God and his revealed will, the Grande Loge de France does not require this reference'. http://www.gldf.org/fr/qui-sommes-nous/les-questions-que-vous-vous-posez?start=6 (accessed February 20, 2015). Nothing could be clearer!

ciety[9] and only preclude them from ending with votes.[10] Finally, it is publicly known that it has always opened its temples to all Brothers from the different French Obediences. Nevertheless, and importantly with regard to the Basel Affair, despite these flagrant contradictions with the Anglo-Saxon definition of regularity, the GLDF, particularly from 2012 to 2014, never stopped claiming the most unquestionable Masonic regularity! This proved that the word was being used to mean something entirely different. Some people realised this, but others did not.

But there is more. Although other Obediences generally do not claim regularity in their official documents, they are far from scorning it in ordinary Masonic conversation. A few examples can be cited.

While I was taking part in a roundtable filmed by Baglis TV (a French Internet TV channel) in 2014, the Grand Mistress of the Grande Loge féminine de France (GLFF: Women's Grand Lodge of France) heard one of the speakers, a member of the Grande Loge nationale française (GLNF), politely say in her presence that women's Masonry could not be regular in the strictest sense of the term. She was immediately offended and answered with great dignity that she took it as an insult not to be 'recognised as such'—that is, as a 'regular Mason'.

When the Grande Loge traditionnelle et symbolique Opéra (GLTSO) was founded in 1958 by Brothers who had left the GLNF, it published a founding manifesto with a very lofty tone. It made absolutely no renunciation of regularity, and it even more skillfully turned a tradi-

---

[9] Though article 23 of its current *Constitutions* explicitly forbids 'political and religious discussions'.

[10] Article IV of the GLDF's *Déclaration de principes* (Declaration of Principles) in 1953.

tional vocabulary on its head, going so far as to define being 'a free Mason in a free Lodge' as the 'landmark of all landmarks'!

Allow me to cite once again, if only for the anecdote, the tiny but most respected Loge nationale française (LNF), which itself emerged in 1968 out of its forbear. In a text written in around 1970 by its founder, René Guilly, it fiercely asserted its meticulous respect of the *Basic Principles* as proof of its regularity. This was true, except for the matter of intervisiting.

Finally, the last to come to the French Masonic landscape, the Grande Loge de l'Alliance maçonnique Française (GL-AMF)—its persistent presence is the only concrete result of the Basel Affair—which is today situated between two worlds, not knowing whether it has renounced the first (the regular, Anglo-Saxon Masonic world from which it came) but unsure about its definitive integration into the second (the French Masonic world in general), is still trying to decide about its regularity, attempting to redefine it. It has even tried to clarify it by consulting a French 'leading historian', who, like a modern-day Solomon, willingly furnished us with his own definition of regularity: the Anglo-Saxon regularity to which he had long belonged, but purged of everything that did not suit him personally ...

This is the fundamental essence of the French paradox of Masonry in France: it considers itself entirely 'regular', and consequently, this word has come to mean very little it the country.

This essentialization of the concept of regularity, notwithstanding the historical circumstances of its appearance and evolution, now entirely neglected, produces a 'catch-all' word that implicitly refers to other values, in particular authenticity. The word 'regular' (*régulier*) is used to mean: 'We are a *true* Masonry.' So understandably, all (or almost all) Obediences claim to be regular!

There is also the idea of an uninterrupted lineage, with its roots in the oldest sources of Freemasonry. This is the obsession with legitimacy expressed by the word 'regularity': in a country that is marked, *horresco referens*, by the old Catholic morality of 'pure and untainted' lineage, it is telling that in the eighteenth century 'irregular' Lodges were often called 'bastard' Lodges.

We can also see that certain people casually or opportunistically confuse such vaguely defined regularity with 'tradition' (more or less imagined and reconstructed according to the needs of the cause) or 'spirituality' (as vague as it is reassuring), provided that it is most importantly neither 'religious' nor 'dogmatic'! So many words to say so little.

In France, in the end, the issue is not so much that the word *régulier* (regular)—and even less so what it means so unambiguously in Great Britain and the United States—is especially attractive; it is above all that the adjective *irrégulier* (irregular) causes annoyance, frustration, and anger on the part of those to whom it is applied.

Consequently, we could end these vocabulary disputes in an instant if we were to forbid the use of the word 'regular' and if we simply agreed that everyone is a Mason in his or her own way, that there are therefore many Obediences with sometimes very different (and even nearly or clearly incompatible) Masonic positions, and that this diversity creates divides between them, even on an international level.

But there it is: almost everyone has decided to express the situation by saying that we are all 'regular' in our way!

In order to get a clearer understanding, we therefore need a little linguistics and a lot of history.

CHAPTER 2

A LITTLE VOCABULARY

Since, in their Masonic application, the words 'regular' and 'regularity' emerged in England from the very beginnings of organised Freemasonry, we must start by looking at English semantics.

What does 'regular' mean in English?

We will use the *Oxford English Dictionary* as our reference here[11]—an unsurpassable authority on English lexicography.

In the long entry devoted to the word 'regular', there are naturally some meanings shared by the French word *régulier*: the character of that which is uniform; without asperity or asymmetry; the repetition of certain events at a fixed rhythm or frequency; and also a regular cleric as opposed to a secular cleric. However, there is an additional meaning that is specific to English: that which conforms to an established and recognised norm—in a word, 'normal'! The only French meaning for the word *régulier* that comes close to this and that is also used in English applies to a *soldat régulier* or 'regular soldier', as opposed to a mercenary who is a *soldat irrégulier* or an 'irregular soldier'. This means that they are not a part of the *armée régulière* or 'regular army', the official army—one hardly dares say, the 'normal army'.

An essential notion emerges here, and a look back at the first historical uses of the word 'regular' in the Masonic universe will confirm it later: we must not give in to the

---

[11] Compact Edition (Oxford University Press, 1971–1987).

very French temptation, explained simultaneously by the information in a dictionary of our modern language and the ecclesiastical traditions of our country (!), of immediately connecting the word *régulier* (regular) with *règle* (rule).[12] After all, Anglo-Saxon Freemasons never make this connection.[13] The word 'regular' therefore simply distinguishes 'normal' Masons, who conform to the current status and who recognise the official authority, from the irregular Masons who do not have a normal and habitual status.

Once again, and I emphasise this, the most common meaning of the English word 'regular' is 'banal, frequent, standard'. This extends well beyond Freemasonry, and is seen in many circumstances in daily life! For example, the sizes used for certain clothes—in length rather than width—in England are: 'short', 'regular' and 'long'. Finally, forgive me for briefly breaking with the seriousness of this study by reminding readers that we can also find condoms in all English drugstores in two sizes: 'regular'—for most users—and 'king size', for a certain few.

Yet in a dictionary of modern French, this precise sense for the word *régulier* is not listed. Nor does it appear in the *Littré*, the largest French lexicography of the nine-

---

[12] And in particular monastic 'rule'. A world that the English abolished from 1536.

[13] The fact that the French 'regular' Obedience, the GLNF, formulated a twelve-point rule (*Règle en douze points*), only adopted in 1968 and reformulating the essentials of the *Basic Principles*, in this respect reveals an approach and an intention that we can respect but that are certainly not in line with the original sense of the word 'regular' when it was first introduced into the Masonic context. We will examine this further later on. One might even say that most English or American Freemasons would find any connection between the Masonic world, the Lodge and a monastery or convent rather puzzling, if not laughable.

teenth century. We can just barely find, in the only sense of the word applicable to people, the idea of 'that which conforms to moral duties', a nuance that does not convey the English meaning of 'regular' that interests us. Similarly, it does not appear in a classical French dictionary (seventeenth and eighteenth centuries). These indications lead us to a highly significant linguistic observation.

The word 'regular', directly translated into French as *régulier*, is in fact what we call a 'false friend': it automatically brings to mind a meaning that is not the same, or not exactly the same, as that of the original word in the source language. Another example is 'actually', which means 'really' in English but suggests 'currently' (*actuellement*) to a French speaker. Similarly, to 'deceive' does not have the same meaning as the French *décevoir* (to disappoint). It seems that the passage from English to French in the little world of Masonry, which is about the only context to have taken on this specific usage of the word 'regular', can only lead to misunderstandings.

All of this must seem self-evident to English-speaking readers. Nevertheless, I wanted to keep this passage from the French version of this book to help them to understand the difficulty of dealing with what is, at the end of the day, a rather simple Masonic problem, when we employ words whose very meaning has been distorted.

Let us now move forward with our investigation.

CHAPTER 3
MADE IN ENGLAND

In Régulier Order?

B ecause (like it or not) it all began in England almost three centuries ago, we should turn to the oldest Masonic texts of the first Grand Lodge 'of London and of Westminster', founded in 1717, in our search for the first elements of the debate.

The emergence of a Grand Lodge claiming superiority over all 'particular' Lodges, which rapidly and evocatively came to be called 'subordinate Lodges', was not without its difficulties: it was in fact a huge innovation in the history of the Craft. This is evidenced by the many resistance attempts right from the start, not only from Lodges that had long refused to follow London, but also from others such as the York Lodge, which asserted (without any entirely convincing proof) its long-established roots and from 1725 called itself the 'Grand Lodge of All England at York'! Of course (and this will be further examined below), we cannot go any further without mentioning the great dispute that truly shaped the whole history of English Masonry from 1751 to 1813: that between the Antients and the Moderns, pitching the first Grand Lodge of 1717 against that founded in London by immigrants of Irish origin. The question of Masonic Obedience, with 'obedience' taken in its strictest sense (Who do we obey?) therefore lay at the centre of English Masonic life throughout the eighteenth century, and its epilogue came in 1813 with the creation of the United Grand Lodge.

It is in this context that we must understand the first notion of regularity: in the eighteenth century, in England, a regular Lodge accepted the authority of a Grand Lodge—and paid fees to it! This entitled its members to solidarity from this Grand Lodge, which was a major Masonic concern at the time, as evidenced by the 1724 creation of the Committee of Charity by the Moderns.

We should remember that at the time Freemasonry in no way defined itself as an 'initiatory and traditional Order', or anything of the sort, but above all as a Brotherhood of men who were united around general principles of Christian morality, were loyal to the civil authorities, were committed to helping and assisting each other in all circumstances of life.

In this context, the *General Regulations* published in 1723[14] gave a fairly clear definition of regularity:

> VIII. If any set or Number of Masons shall take upon themselves to form a *Lodge* without the Grand Master's Warrant, the *regular Lodges* are not to countenance them, or own them as *fair brethren* and duly form'd, nor approve of their Acts and Deeds; but must treat them as *Rebels*, until they humble themselves, as the *Grand Master*, shall, in his Prudence, direct, and until he approve of them by his *Warrant*, which must be signified to the *other Lodges*, as the Custom is when a *new* Lodge is to be registered in the *List of Lodges*. [15]

The 1738 edition also mentions two decisions taken by

---

[14] But fixed from 1720 following the instructions of George Payne, Grand Master.

[15] James Anderson, *The Constitutions of the Freemasons* (London, 1723), 60.

the Grand Lodge in 1724 and included in the new edition of the *General Regulations*:

> On February 19, 1724.
>
> None who form a *Stated Lodge* without the *Grand Master's* Leave, shall be admitted into *regular* Lodges, till they make Submission and obtain Grace.
>
> On Tuesday, November 21, 1724.
>
> If any Brethren *form a Lodge* without Leave, and shall irregularly make *new*[16] Brothers, they shall not be admitted into any *regular Lodge*, no not as *Visitors*, till they render a good Reason, or make due Submission.[17]

It is clear that regularity at the time was essentially, if not exclusively, an administrative and perhaps disciplinary matter. The 'irregulars' had simply not been authorised by the Grand Master to make a Lodge, and this meant that their Lodge could not appear on the highly official List of Lodges—the only Lodges whose members had the right to mutual assistance from the Fraternity. However, if they were to repent ('humble themselves', 'make Submission', or provide a 'good Reason!'), then the Grand Master would undoubtedly display the paternal goodwill to approve them. This would make them regular without further ado. All they ever needed to do was recognise the authority of the only Grand Lodge.

---

[16] In the original text, the italics emphasize the word 'new': these irregular Brothers were actually trying to impose a new burden on the others in the name of fraternal solidarity, without their consent (expressed by a warrant from the Grand Master), and this was the fundamental accusation against them.

[17] James Anderson, *The New Book of Constitutions* (London, 1738), 156.

This was an important matter. Even just by browsing the book of minutes from the Grand Lodge from 1723 onwards, we can see that most of the debates concerned the registration of new Lodges and the attribution of benevolence funds. In fact, these were two faces of the same problem.

At a Grand Lodge meeting on February 24, 1735, it was even decided:

> That no extraneous Brothers, that is, not regularly made, but clandestinely, or only with a View to partake of the Charity, nor any assisting and such irregular Makings, shall ever by qualified to partake of the Masons general Charity.[18]

Administrative regularity and the right to benevolence were therefore inseparable in this early English Freemasonry. No other concern played a part.

We should note that in everything described above, the notion of 'recognition' does not yet appear to be connected to that of regularity. 'Recognition', in this old context, refers only to the procedure used to ensure that one is definitely in the presence of a Freemason. Thus, in England, young initiates are still taught the modes of recognition: the sign, the token and the word of their degree.

This underlies the Masonic formula constantly repeated since those times:

> Q. Are you a Freemason? A. My brothers recognize me as such.[19]

---

[18] Ibid. 182.

[19] This now classic exchange is first seen in a French text, the 1744 *Catéchisme des francs-maçons*. Nevertheless, all British catechisms from the late seventeenth to the early eighteenth century feature

However, if it is possible today to be a 'regular' Mason (or presumed to be one) and not (yet) recognised', it is no exaggeration to say that in the eighteenth century, the reverse was true: it was possible to be entirely 'recognised' as a Freemason, without necessarily being 'regular'.

Recognition at the time was purely a personal affair and did not affect a person's Masonic identity (confirmed or not). And of course, it was not yet a matter of recognising another Grand Lodge.

Above all, another point must be emphasised, because today, it lies at the heart of contemporary debates about regularity: in the eighteenth century, people searched in vain for a philosophical or religious definition of regularity.

The standards of Masonry had been summarised in the *Constitutions* of 1723, and related to its 'metaphysical' foundations in General Head I of the *Charges of a Freemason.* I will not recap here the endless discussions concerning the actually rather simple interpretation of this text, a matter that I have addressed elsewhere.[20] To summarise an analysis that I find hard to contest, it remains that a Freemason at this time was required to believe in God and to respect religious duties (which were above all moral), but he chose his own religion freely, and this could not be a matter for dispute with his other Brothers. However, we should remember that the word 'regular' during Anderson's time in no way referred to adherence or non-adherence to this view of Masonry: there was no alternative view!

---

exactly equivalent formulas, even though the words 'recognition' and 'recognize' do not yet feature.

[20] Particularly in a note on my blog (in French): http://pierresvivantes. hautetfort.com/archive/2015/01/04/la-franc-maconnerie-et-elle-theiste-deiste-ou-adogmatique-5526200.html.

Although 'free' Masons and Lodges neglected or refused, sometimes for several centuries, to place themselves under the Obedience of a Grand Lodge (not considering it remotely necessary to Freemasonry), it was never for reasons of 'freedom of conscience' that the 1723 *Constitutions* were supposedly violated! In Great Britain in the early eighteenth century, everyone agreed on these fundamental principles of Christianity. Those who rebelled against this vision of the world could be counted on the fingers of one hand, and it is clear that the fundamental texts of Masonry did not welcome such individuals.

In other words, a regular Mason in eighteenth century England was not a 'dogmatic' Mason who opposed 'liberal' Freemasonry, as we would say in France today. This comparison would have meant nothing to Masons at this time. Moreover, after over 150 years of bloody political and religious conflicts, the formula of harmony proposed by the 1723 text—entirely in the spirit of the Toleration Act[21] of 1689, after the Glorious Revolution and the destitution of the Stuarts—was in fact seen as great progress, and like all Englishmen of his time, this is the meaning that Anderson gave to the expression 'Liberty of Conscience' in the 1738 edition:[22] it referred notably to the right to choose one's religion in peace![23]

---

[21] Enacted by the Parliament, and approved by the Sovereign, the *Toleration Act* established total freedom of belief for all Protestants, provided that they recognize the authorities in power, but it now deprived most Catholics, Unitarians (those rejecting the Trinitarian doctrine) and Atheists of most of their civil and political rights. Naturally, this was still effective in legislation in 1723.

[22] *Dedication*, V.

[23] This also shows how far the interpretation sometimes proposed of the 1738 *Constitutions*, which considers them a 'dogmatic' step backwards compared to those of 1723, is the result of a profound misunderstanding of the intellectual and religious history of

From 1726 to 1729, the young Voltaire, temporarily exiled to London, was not fooled. In his *Lettres philosophiques*, published in 1734, he describes in particular what he saw as the admirable spectacle of a country where the fullest religious freedom went hand in hand with the fervent but peaceful commitment of every religious community to its beliefs and values. He wrote,

> Take a view of the Royal Exchange in London, a place more venerable than many courts of justice, where the representatives of all nations meet for the benefit of mankind. There the Jew, the Mahometan, and the Christian transact together, as though they all profess'd the same religion, and give the name of Infidel to none but bankrupts. There the Presbyterian confides in the Anabaptist, and the Churchman depends on the Quaker's word. Breaking up of this pacific and free assembly, some withdraw to the synagogue, and others take a glass. This man goes and is baptiz'd in a great tub, in the name of the Father, Son, and the Holy Ghost: That man has his son's foreskin cut off, whilst a sett of Hebrew words (quite unintelligible to him) are mumbled over his child. Others retire to their churches and there wait for the inspiration of heaven with their hats on, and all are satisfied.
>
> If one religion only were allowed in England, the Government would very possibly become arbitrary; if there were but two, the people wou'd cut one another's throats; but as there are such a multitude, they all live happy and in peace.[24]

England at this time.

[24] Letter VI, 'On the Presbyterians'.

In this text, where humour only steps aside to leave room for pertinent observation, simply replacing 'Royal Exchange in London' with 'Masonic Lodge' would give us a fairly accurate portrayal of the atmosphere of English Masonry in around 1730.

Remaking a Mason

Things changed somewhat with the creation, mentioned above, of a second Grand Lodge in England in 1751. Now that a new Masonic power was attempting to exert its control on English territory, conflict with the first Grand Lodge was inevitable, and the stakes were considerable: Masonic supremacy, and perhaps, for one or the other of the Grand Lodges, long-term survival.

This was when a Masonic practice that would continue until the Union in 1813 appeared: the remaking of a Mason. When a Brother, initiated into a Lodge that was part of one of the Grand Lodges, wanted to change 'Obedience'[25] for whatever reason (often just a personal dispute), he was generally required to be 'remade' or reinitiated as a Mason. This implied that he had not truly been one before! This Mason was 'irregular' and not truly a Mason in the eyes of the Grand Lodge that he sought to join. He needed 'remaking'. However, as we have seen, when an 'irregular' or 'clandestine' Mason presented himself to the authorities of the first Grand Lodge, he would simply be required to offer explanations and submit. Generally, he would not be reinitiated.

So what was the difference between a 'Modern' Mason

[25] Some changed several times in both directions! This coming and going undoubtedly played a role in the progressive homogenization of practices between Lodges on the two sides.

(First Grand Lodge of 1717) and an 'Antient'[26] Mason? Once again, we cannot cover this whole subject here, especially as in certain Masonic circles in France it has been subject to extremely biased and often politically motivated interpretations, and because recent research in England leads us to see the matter in a new light.[27] Nevertheless, we can say that although the Antients accused the Moderns of all kinds of turpitudes, reproaching them when necessary for changing a ritual in ways not been clearly confirmed by evidence, the purely Masonic differences between the two families were certainly not as significant as has been claimed.

Of course, there were differences in the layout of the Lodge, the arrangement of symbols, and the details of ceremonies, but it is worth emphasising that the general mindset of the two Grand Lodges was almost the same, particularly concerning the religious foundations of the Masonic ritual, a true commonplace in English society at the time, and therefore in Masonry itself. Given this, it is easy to understand how, despite 60 years of rivalry, the union of the two powers in 1813 was so easy.

At the end of the day, remaking was more a shaming, a slightly humiliating obligation placed upon a past rebel who had been converted to better sentiments, than any sign of real intellectual, philosophical, or religious difference between the two Grand Lodges. Nevertheless, the two notions of regularity and recognition, initially very distinct and not directly related, had begun to cross over somewhat.

---

[26] The form 'Antient' is used consistently by English Masonic historians.

[27] It was above all social and economic characteristics, rather than intellectual differences, that separated the two groups. See in particular Ric Berman, *Schism: The Battle that Forged Freemasonry* (Brighton, UK: Sussex Academic Press, 2013).

Charter of Compact

Shortly after the Union of 1813, the young UGLE sealed an agreement with the two other Grand Lodges in the British Isles (those of Scotland and Ireland), which had long opposed the Grand Lodge of the Moderns and preferred to maintain connections with the Antients. The aim was to take into account the new situation created by the Union. This Charter of Compact was a general agreement specifying (among other things) the status of the naturally itinerant military Lodges, which the three powers had set up around the world.

In order to regulate their relationships with the sedentary, civil lodges, the three Home Grand Lodges agreed that

> [these Lodges] shall be *recognised*, visited, and have the right of visitation and intercourse with the *regular* Lodges [meaning the civil Lodges of the three Grand Lodges], where it may happen to be.[28]

Once again, the text shows that 'regular' and 'recognised' were still just used to refer to Lodges that conformed administratively with their respective Grand Lodges and the Brothers in them.

However, in the meantime, Freemasonry had crossed the Channel to France. How would regularity be seen in this emerging French Masonry?

---

[28] Irish copy published in R.E. Parkinson, *History of the Grand Lodge of Ireland*, Lodge of research CC, Dublin, 1957, 20–24.

CHAPTER 4

REGULARITY IN EIGHTEENTH-CENTURY FRANCE

In France as in London!

We know that the first Freemasons in France were British immigrants, but they had not come for the pleasure of setting up Freemasonry in France. Their leader, Derwentwater, who created the so-called St. Thomas Lodge on Rue des Boucheries in Paris, actually did not want to let Frenchmen join! These British immigrants in fact came for political and religious reasons. They included many Jacobites, supporters of the Stuart dynasty, which had been driven from the throne.

We do not know when and where most of these 'founding Brothers' were initiated. Nevertheless, their political position allows us to consider them 'irregular' in more ways than one, since the Lodges from which they came did not recognise the authority of the Grand Lodge in London, which was Hanoverian and loyal to the authorities in power: their sworn enemies.[29] In the early days of Parisian Masonry, there was a sort of competition between 'Gallican' and 'Anglican' Lodges, to use the terms that were popularised by French historian Pierre Chevallier[30] but go back to the works of Gustave Bord,[31] which seem to me not entirely pertinent.

---

[29] Derwentwater was beheaded in London in 1746, and died a martyr to the Catholic and Stuart cause.

[30] Pierre Chevallier, *Histoire de la franc-maçonnerie française*, 3 vols. (Paris: Fayard, 1974).

[31] Gustave Bord, *La Franc-maçonnerie en France, des origines à 1815*, vol. 1 (Paris: Nouvelle librairie nationale, 1908).

Still, the Au Louis d'Argent Lodge, which historians sometimes call St. Thomas II and which followed on from (or took the place of) that founded by Derwentwater, was recognised by the Grand Lodge of London in 1732 and features on the list of its Lodges from 1735. A witness at the time even called it 'the most regular in France'! And so, from the first days of French Masonry, the great word was already being used.

From the evidence, it again appears that the French adjective *régulière* when applied to a Lodge cannot in this case have referred to the administrative act of obedience to London. Knowing whether the 'Gallican' Lodges (reputed to be under the Jacobite influence) and the 'Anglican' Lodges (supposedly of strictly Hanoverian obedience) had tangibly different Masonic practices is a false problem. Aside from the endlessly repeated reference to the introduction of the sword into the Lodge by the Count of Derwentwater, which caused a stir in Paris in 1737 before becoming a French custom that was unanimously adopted and observed throughout the century, no 'Jacobite' ritual had so far differed significantly from its supposedly 'Hanoverian' equivalent.

However, from René Hérault's revelations in the 1737 *La Réception d'un Frey-Maçon*, the first description of French Masonic customs, to the 1751 *Maçon démasqué*, we have access to a rather homogeneous set of texts. We can therefore state fairly certainly that the Masonic ritual for the first three degrees from 1742 to 1750 was for the most part identical (apart from a few inevitable local variants) in France and England, or at least in Paris and London, and that it represented the fundamental nucleus of what would later be called the tradition of the Moderns.

Consequently, the word *régulier* still came into French Masonic discourse in the eighteenth century in its primarily administrative sense. Once again, it took time for the Grand Lodge of Paris, 'supposedly of France', to establish a semblance of authority over the whole kingdom. Even in 1760, in the traditional Gallic capital, a 'Grand Lodge of Regular Masters of Lyon' formed, showing little willingness to bow to the Parisian authority. This explains the title taken by Count Louis of Clermont when he became Grand Master in 1743: 'Grand Master of the Regular Lodges of France',[32] rather than 'Grand Master of the Grand Lodge of France'. Even in 1771, the Duke of Chartres would be called 'Grand Master and Protector of all the Regular Lodges of France'.[33]

So what attitude did the Grand Lodge of London (later of England) adopt in the face of this French claim to both regularity and autonomy?

The first reaction that we can record is that seen in the 1738 edition of the *Constitutions*. Whereas, London had given warrants to Parisian Lodges, for example the Aubigny-Richmond Lodge,[34] a few years later Anderson observed that

> all these Lodges are under the Patronage of our
> Grand Master of England;
>
> But the *old Lodge* at York City and the *Lodges*

---

[32] *Statuts de la loge St Jean de Jérusalem*, Lodge of the Grand Master in Paris, in 1745 and 1755.

[33] *Statuts et Règlement de la Très Respectable Grande Loge de France* (article XIII).

[34] Presided over by the Duke of Richmond, who was Grand Master from 1724 to 1725 in London, following on from the Duke of Wharton, himself later recognized as Grand Master in France in 1728.

of Scotland, Ireland, France, and Italy, affecting Independency, are under their own *Grand
Masters*; tho' they have the same *constitutions,
charges, regulations* &c. for substance, with
their Brethren of England, and are equally zeal-
ous for the *Augustan Stile*, and the *secrets* of the
antient and honorable *fraternity*.[35]

Basically, however authoritative (or not) we can consider this text; Anderson admits in it the existence of now
autonomous Grand Lodges. He therefore does not call
them 'irregular' and even emphasises that their constitutional and regulatory foundations conform entirely to
the English customs. He does not dwell on the subject
further, and does not mention the conditions to be ful-
filled or propose a definition to be respected for 'regular
Masonry'. In fact, the very expression did not yet exist.

Consequently, we can see that the question of international relations began with a very peaceful observation.

It was in fact so true that article VIII of the *General Regulations* of 1723, cited above, was fully and faithfully translated in article 16 of the *Règlements généraux* adopted in
Paris on 11 December, 1743.[36]

French Masonic life throughout the eighteenth century
saw clashes between organizations aspiring to supremacy
over a wide variety of degrees. This scene was infinitely
more complex than that seen in England at the same time.
However, every time the word for 'regularity' was used in
France, it was simply to describe the legitimacy and authority being claimed over another Masonic body, whose

[35] Anderson, *The New Book of Constitutions*, 196.

[36] Cited in Alain Bernheim, 'Contribution à la connaissance de la
genèse de la première Grande Loge de France,' *Villard de Honne-
court* 17 (1988): 128.

power or origins were being contested, and which was sometimes also described as 'schismatic' or 'apocryphal'.

For its part, when the Grand Lodge of England created links with other Grand Lodges established in other countries, it never spoke of 'recognition', though it sometimes exchanged guarantees of friendship. These were the limits of international Masonic relations until the mid-nineteenth century. Throughout the eighteenth century, a Mason travelling in Europe would show his diploma or 'Grand Lodge Certificate', as it was called in England, and on the whole, he would be received without any mention of the 'regularity' issue in the sense attached to it today: he was attached to a Grand Lodge, and that was enough. In the event of doubt, he would be traditionally examined. At this time, there was a true 'European Masonic space'—and even a global one if we include the American colonies.

The Infancy of Masonic Diplomacy

In 1765, the Grand Lodge of the Moderns even made a treaty with the first Grand Lodge of France. It simply stipulated that neither would create Lodges on the other's territory: an agreement that England quickly broke by giving patents in 1766 to the Anglaise Lodge in Bordeaux (although this was founded in 1732) and also to Lodges in Le Havre and Grenoble![37]

In order to establish its hegemony in France, the Grand

---

[37] Pierre-Yves Beaurepaire, 'Quand les francs-maçons signent des traités diplomatiques: circulations et échanges maçonniques entre France et Angleterre (1765–1775),' in *Cultural Transfers: France and Britain in the Long Eighteenth Century*, eds. Ann Thomson et al. (Oxford: Voltaire Foundation, 2010), 74–75.

Orient de France, created in 1773, reworked the two notions of 'regularity' and 'recognition'—with regard to Brothers—in its *Statuts de l'Ordre royal de franc-maçonnerie en France* of May 24, 1773:

ARTICLE I

The body of the Royal Order of Freemasonry, under the distinctive title of Masonic Body of France, will be composed only of Regular Masons, recognized as such by the Grand Orient.

ARTICLE II

The Grand Orient de France will henceforth only recognize Members of Regular Lodges as Regular Masons.

ARTICLE III

The Grand Orient de France will henceforth only recognize as Regular Lodges those with Constitutions accorded or renewed by the Grand Orient; which alone will have the rights to deliver these.

It is clear that in adopting the notions of recognition and regularity, the Grand Orient made no distinction between them. The message is simple and 'circular': the Grand Orient only recognises regular Masons, and regular Masons are those recognised by the Grand Orient, because they are members of Lodges that it recognises, which for this very reason are regular Lodges! We might search in vain for any indication as to the philosophical meaning of this 'regularity', and it is interesting to note that until 1849 the GODF saw no use in having a text summarising its basic views regarding the very nature of the Masonic institution. Nevertheless, we are left with these official rituals, which give us useful information: for it was these rituals, and not the administrative texts, that were used to make Masons!

In practice, for the Grand Orient, regular Lodges were those willing to recognise its authority and pay their dues, which were often heavy.

But what can be said of its position regarding England? In 1775, there was a project for a treaty between the Grand Lodge of the Moderns and the young Grand Orient de France[38]—the institutional heir of the first Grande Loge de France. This treaty was never concluded. However, the cause of this failure was far from philosophical: the Grand Secretary of England, Heseltine, in particular judged the formulation of article 1 of the Grand Orient's proposal inadmissible:

> the intention of the g[rand] o[rient] de france
> is to agree with that of London, equal to equal,
> this equality which must form the basis for the
> treaty of union.[39]

However, the decision also focused greatly on England's reluctance to make its French foundations join the Grand Orient. Therefore, the project failed because of a difference of precedence and not a 'doctrinal' dispute (in fact, this was never evoked). Nevertheless, it is worth emphasising in passing, as playfully observed by Alain Bernheim[40] (who remains a great researcher despite himself),

---

[38] But not with the 'maintained' Grand Lodge or 'Grand Orient of Clermont', which disappeared in 1799, merging with the Grand Orient.

[39] Beaurepaire, 'Quand les francs-maçons signent des traités diplomatiques', 79.

[40] Alain Bernheim, *Une Certaine idée de la franc-maçonnerie* (Paris: Dervy, 2008), 46–47.

one year after its creation, the United Grand Lodge had 647 lodges; whereas the Grand Orient de France had 886: 'equality' favoured France!

Despite this, under the First Empire, with war raging between the two countries, some French officers, all members of the Grand Orient de France imprisoned on English pontoons and wanting to 'regularly' form a Lodge, requested and obtained a surprising warrant from the Masonic authorities. The first lines of the document tell us much about Masonic views at the time:

> In the Name and under the Auspices of the Grand Orient of France,
>
> And under the immediate protection of His Lordship, the very powerful, very illustrious and very worshipful Brother Lord Moira, Acting Grand Master of all the Regular Lodges of the Kingdom of Great Britain.[41]

Thus, England never had any official relationship with the Grand Orient de France, because this was not customary. Even right in the middle of a merciless war, however, this in no way prevented each side fully 'recognising' the 'regular' Masonic nature of the other! According to these old customs, French Brothers were received in English Lodges during the nineteenth century—and in some cases still after 1877. In 1875, a polite exchange of letters even took place between the president of the GODF General Council and the UGLE Grand Secretary, when the Prince of Wales, the future Edward VII, became Grand Master. It was only a formal and sociable exchange with no commitments made, but it did at least prove that the

---

[41] John Thorp, *French Prisoners Lodges* (Leicester, UK: Bro. George Gibbons, 1900), 88.

two sides could talk.[42]

It suffices to say, before mentioning the event that is in everyone's minds—the famous 1877 convent—that on this occasion the United Grand Lodge of England therefore never resolved to break ties that had not been officially sanctioned by any treaty!

A careful re-examination of the buildup to this affair, as well as its political and social environment and its consequences, is necessary here, if we are to understand the situation at the time.

---

[42] *Bulletin du GODF* (1875), 173–174. Strangely, in his answer, the English Grand Secretary expresses his Grand Master's wish (who for many reasons was a great Francophile, as we know!) that 'the good relationships that have so long existed between the two nations should characterize the Grand Lodges of France and England'. This was either an overstatement or an understatement: it would be another thirty or so years before an *entente cordiale* was reached, after the 1898 Fashoda incident, which took us right to the verge of a war; the good Masonic relationships are seen here more as a wish than as reality.

CHAPTER 5

THE 1877 CONVENT AFFAIR

The Great Turning Point in French Masonry

I do not propose here to retrace the history of a convent (congress) that has already been widely studied, and of which the conclusions are (or should be) very well known.

I would simply like to remind readers of the essential point: the Grand Orient did not decide in September 1877, as has sometimes been written, to dismiss the 'Great Architect of the Universe'. All it did was modify the text of article 1 of its *Constitution*, which since its first promulgation in 1849 had read,

> Freemasonry, an eminently philanthropic, philosophical, and progressive institution, has as its foundation the existence of God and the immortal soul.

This formula was of course introduced in accordance with a long textual tradition of Freemasonry, but also in the climate of romantic deism and spiritualist socialism that was very popular from 1848 and was met with a certain enthusiasm in France. The 1854 revision added a new element: 'Love of humanity'. However, that of 1865 made the 1849 text less 'dogmatic' with the addition of the following paragraph:

> It [Freemasonry] considers liberty of conscience as a right that belongs to every individual and excludes nobody because of their beliefs.

This new addition already introduced a subtle but undeniable contradiction in terms.

The version adopted by the 1877 convent after a rich debate no longer mentioned the obligation to believe in God and the immortal soul. The rest of the text remained unchanged. Consequently, it was only by an extensive application of this decision that the reference to the GAO-TU gradually disappeared from its internal documents: first from the header and official boards (article 104 of the 1882 *Statuts et Règlements généraux* [General Statutes and Regulations]), then from the new edition of the rituals, which was published in 1887.

Nevertheless, this consequence was quite predictable, and it clearly shows that for Brothers in the late nineteenth century (and particularly for those who no longer wanted it!), the traditional vocabulary of the Great Architect of the Universe had obviously always referred to God in Masonic rituals. And God was essentially seen (even if this was in the most liberal and open way) from the perspective of Judeo-Christian tradition. This was unsurprising, since this religious tradition had been dominant in Europe for centuries, and because it had infused Freemasonry with its symbols, rituals, and customs since its very beginnings.

However, there was still a change in situation (as described in the preceding chapter) from the early nineteenth century, when conventional deism still prevailed in French lodges, to the crisis situation created by the decision of 1877.

The Second Empire marked a turning point for political, economic and social history in France, but also for the country's intellectual and religious history. It was under the Authoritarian Empire (1851–1860) that Lodges in France underwent a definitive sociological mutation (although this actually began several years before). They gradually became the refuge for many thinkers who favored political and social progress, as well as a reduction in the power of the Catholic Church. We should remember that at the time, in the eyes of many French people, these two things were (at least almost) the same battle. In the absence of any other institutional sites (the legislative body was at the time silenced and powerless) or associative sites (political parties had no legal existence) allowing expression of such views, Masonic Lodges (which still had a relatively free status and were 'tolerated by the government') spontaneously brought together the opponents.[43]

Having eventually lost the support of a large part of the Catholic population because of his Italian policy against the Papal States, Napoleon III began the second phase of his reign, the Liberal Empire, from 1860. This was when, freed from some of the institutional obstacles that had formerly silenced it, a certain opinion found a voice. The current of thought that favoured republican ideas gradually became organised, anticlerical discourse was asserted more clearly, and this movement was heard in the Lodges, which were already prepared to welcome and relay it.

In 1852, the Grand Orient, without a Grand Master since the fall of Napoleon I, found a new leader: Prince Murat, the emperor's cousin. We know about the unusual

---

[43] In a way, this is reminiscent of the opposition in American colonies between the Lodges of the Antients (which recruited mainly among the working class and contained many insurgents) and those of the Moderns (which had greater links to the British authorities). It is worth remembering, for example, the role that the members of the St. Andrew Lodge played in the Boston Tea Party.

circumstances in which Marshal Bernard Magnan (who had been one of the players in the 1851 coup d'état) was in turn named 'Grand Master of the Masonic Order' in 1862, by a decree from the emperor, when he was not even a Mason! After receiving the 33 degrees of the Ancient and Accepted Scottish Rite in just two days (a very unusual occurrence in France) and after failing to submit the Supreme Council in France (heroically defended by Grand Commander Viennet) to his power, he resolved to take control of the Grand Orient. However, less well known is the fact that the emperor made this decision in order to deal with the problem of finding a successor to Prince Murat, who had led the Grand Orient despotically. Two years later, after Napoleon III had given the Grand Orient the right to elect its Grand Master, Magnan kept his role without difficulty and acted as a very constitutional Head of the Order until he died.

When Magnan died in 1865, the Archbishop of Paris, Monseigneur Darboy,[44] tolerated the presence of Masonic decorations on the marshal's coffin, as well as his cane, during his funeral at Notre-Dame in Paris. Word of the affair got out and led to an incident with the Vatican. Thus, even in death, the Grand Master, although once forced upon the Masons as leader, suffered the outrage of the Catholic Church with the Brothers.

However, France was not the only country to see such an evolution. In Belgium, which at the time was dominated by a Walloon bourgeoisie who were very sensitive to French influence, the fervent action of the Catholic Church against Masonry meant that only sympathisers of the Liberal Party (a true hotbed of progressivist, rationalist and anti-Catholic action) were able to remain in

---

[44] Who was shot during the Paris Commune uprising in 1871.

the Lodges. From 1871, the Grand Orient de Belgique (GODB); therefore decided to rid its official rituals and documents of any reference to the Great Architect of the Universe, apparently without angering London. What is more, in 1875, the GODB and the UGLE, which until then had been quite distant from each other, established certain connections. In any case, 15 year later, religious historian and (Liberal) politician Goblet d'Alviella, Grand Master of the GODB in 1884, who had played an undeniable role in forging this relationship, received the honour of being elected as a member of the QCCC: the Correspondence Circle of the London Lodge Quatuor Coronati 2076, the 'Holy of Holies' of international Masonic wisdom. He became a member in 1909 and gave several lectures.

Was the UGLE fully aware of the Belgian decision of 1871? Nothing could be less certain: Belgium was not France. And did geopolitical considerations not also come into play? The exact nature and extent of the relationships established at this time, which did not prosper much beyond the First World War, are not made clear in the fragments of correspondence available to us.[45] The case of Belgium thus remains somewhat enigmatic.

It would also be wrong to believe that the march towards rationalism and anticlericalism affected only the GODF in France. A similar evolution was also felt in the symbolic Lodges under the Obedience of the Suprême Conseil de France (SCDF: Supreme Council of France).

From 1865, the first section of the Grande Loge Centrale (the body that, under the aegis of the Supreme Council, was responsible for the blue Lodges at the time) voted 24–28 in favour of a motion stating that belief in God

---

[45] See the citations of Alain Bernheim, AQC 100: 78.

and the immortal soul should be an individual decision. Consequently, the Lodge La Justice no. 133 decided to remove any reference to the Great Architect of the Universe from all its documents.

To make matters worse, in 1869, at a meeting of the Grande Loge Centrale, the conclusions of the rapporteur Brother Thirifoq (who was not really given to moderation and who would later join the revolutionaries at the Paris Commune), were rejected. Against his recommendation, the Lodge decided to remove all references to the Great Architect of the Universe. Adolphe Crémieux, newly elected Grand Commander, and the only confirmed republican in the Supreme Council, introduced a compromise. In new regulations, the 'adoration of the Great Architect of the Universe', was replaced by new principles:

> [The Masonic Order] is based on the principle of religious freedom, on the rules of the purest morality, and on the highest doctrines of philosophy ... Its motto is Liberty, Equality, Fraternity.

In return, a synthesis adopted by the Grande Loge Centrale encouraged 'maintenance of the formula consecrated by our traditions'. The Great Architect had narrowly dodged the bullet that would hit its target eight years later—at the Grand Orient de France!

However, the dispute began again in 1872, and in December 1873 the Supreme Council made one last effort to regain control of its Lodges, several of which had deliberately stopped invoking the Great Architect. A decree reiterated that this was a mandatory part of the Rite: five Parisian Lodges protested and were punished immediately. The respite was short lived: in May 1874, at the Grande

Loge Centrale, the Grand Orator was forced to observe that the Lodges were 'currently overwhelmed by the winds of discord'. These winds would not die down again.

In 1880, this movement would lead to an initial split, with the creation of the Grande Loge Symbolique Ecossaise (Scottish Grand Symbolic Lodge), repudiating the GAO-TU, then the creation of the Grande Loge de France in 1894, with the consent, for better or worse, of the SCDF. However, while asserting its support for the reference to the Great Architect (which would later be a major issue in the eventual creation of the GLDF), there was no longer any question of imposing any form of belief in God, even under a symbolic name.

Later, in 1875, the Convent of Lausanne, a congress mainly made up of the Supreme Councils of Europe, adopted a *Declaration of Principles* that recognised the existence of a 'Creating Principle known as the Great Architect of the Universe'. Without going into the details here, let us say that some of the Anglo-Saxon representatives, several of whom had a poor command (or no command) of the French language used for the debate, initially accepted this wording. However, they later judged it to be ambiguous and inadequate, and eventually renounced it in the following two years. Only Latin countries, with France at the forefront, adopted it. As the Grand Chancellor of the Supreme Council of France, Georges Guiffrey stated:

> This formula is so general and so vague that it leaves the door open for all beliefs and all declarations. It will satisfy both believers and materialists.[46]

---

[46] André Combes, *Histoire de la franc-maçonnerie au XIXème siècle*, vol. II (Monaco: Editions du Rocher, 1999), 176.

This, at the end of the day, was the criticism expressed by the Americans and the British.[47] Consequently, Lausanne ended with the Supreme Councils in disarray regarding the key question[48] of the Great Architect: a name alone was not enough. A definition was required. In France, the Rite Ecossais Ancien et Accepté (Ancient and Accepted Scottish Rite) remained in a state of complete ambiguity, which had temporarily distanced it from the most important Supreme Councils in the world. For the Grand Orient, time was running out.

Finally, it should be noted that in 1875, a few weeks before the Convent of Lausanne but entirely unrelated to it, Emile Littré, national treasure and author of an immortal French-language dictionary, but also a champion of positivism,[49] was initiated into the Clémente Amitié Lodge at the GODF, at the same time as Jules Ferry, future creator of 'secular, free and mandatory' schooling in France. This social event attracted a considerable crowd and eloquently showed the now significant weight of republican and secular ideas in the largest French Obedience.

Now, the great debate could begin.[50]

---

[47] In an amusing (but perhaps also revealing) chronological coincidence, on October 10, 1877, one month after the decision by the GODF convent, and even before the UGLE had officially expressed its profound disagreement (see below), the Supreme Council Of England, in the context of a long and complicated dispute following the Convent of Lausanne, asked that the expression 'Creating Principle', stipulated in the *Declaration of Principles*, be replaced by 'Supreme Creator', which was much less ambiguous!

[48] Territorial matters were another important subject of dispute.

[49] A Catholic bishop, Monseigneur Dupanloup, resigned dramatically from the French Academy when it elected the author of the famous dictionary.

[50] The best, most factual, and least biased summary of this now mythical event, even if it is dated in some ways, is still Daniel Ligou, *Frédéric Desmons et la franc-maçonnerie sous la IIIème République*

'Do Not Fear Our Isolation within the Masonic World'

From 1865, there were proposals to revise article 1 of the 1849 *Constitution*, but none made it before the congress. The decision to put to such a project to the Lodges only came in 1876, with a ruling to be made the following year.

On September 9, 1877, Frédéric Desmons, future president of the Council of the Order and then pastor of the Reformed Church (a position that he only left in 1881),[51] was made rapporteur for the resolution. In a long and elegant speech, he methodically but calmly refuted the arguments that could go against the proposed reform: it lay open to criticism from enemies of the Grand Orient, who represented it as a hideout for 'materialists and atheists';[52] it created the risk of a 'schism' in a Grand Orient itself; and it put the Grand Orient in danger of 'isolation within universal Masonry'.

On this last point, Desmons's extremely weak counterargument was that the Grand Orient would not be the first to take this path, citing as precedents the 'Grand Lodge of Buenos Aires', the 'Grand Lodge that has just formed in Hungary', and the 'Grand Orient of Italy'. All of these Obediences were strongly committed to a Masonic path

---

(Paris: Gedalge, 1966), 79–95.

[51] Nevertheless, from this time, this very liberal Protestant fought resolutely as a 'left-wing' radical, in a political career that would lead him to become vice president of the Senate from 1902 to 1906. At the request of his electors, he gave up his pastoral position. In 1910, his 'purely civil' funeral was a key event in political life, particularly in his stronghold in Gard, but for local Protestant circles, it was 'cause for a scandal'.

[52] From the year before, the GODF authorities had rejected the idea that it wanted to 'profess atheism', and 'give its Constitution an element of negation that would create an equally severe danger for liberty of conscience and tolerance'. (Ligou, *Frédéric Desmons et la franc-maçonnerie,* 83).

that already differed greatly from that of the Anglo-Saxons! What is more, in this speech, he said nothing about London and simply offered a (naïve, sincere, or too political?) reassurance:

> Do not worry, my Brothers, do not fear our isolation within the Masonic world.[53]

What followed was a cruel demonstration of how wrong he was.

The proposal went to the vote easily, and although we do not know the exact results, Desmons himself stated that out of the 210 Lodges who sent their preliminary reports to the Grand Orient, more than two-thirds voted for the proposal. The idea was therefore clearly approved with a very comfortable majority, in accordance with the rapporteur's recommendations.

This was a key moment in the history of the English definition of the notions of regularity and recognition. This was the moment when, for the very first time, the English decided to make these ideas more specific.

We have seen the impossibility of considering the 1877 convent without taking into account the political, intellectual and religious background in France under the Second Empire. It is equally impossible to understand the English reaction in 1877 without examining the journey of English Freemasonry since the 1813 union and the end of the Napoleonic Wars.

Don't Give In for an Empire

In many respects, as concerns its own institutional evo-

---

[53] Ligou, *Frédéric Desmons et la franc-maçonnerie*, 88.

lution, English Masonry had taken almost the opposite path to French Masonry, in a political and religious environment almost diametrically opposed to that of France. More precisely, it pursued its initial trajectory without problems to a completion of sorts. One might almost say that in the 1870s, English Masons were not far from thinking that their Masonry had achieved a sort of perfection. We should neither be offended by this and nor should we mock it. Instead, we should try to understand: London's reactions to the French decision of 1877 in fact appear entirely natural.

Following the end of the Napoleonic regime in France, victorious England entered a new phase of its history. Freed from a long conflict that might have threatened its existence, and now ruler of the seas, it was about to build an empire. In the fabulous rise that the country experienced throughout the nineteenth century, British society was able to rely on three profoundly united pillars. The first of these was the monarchy (now firmly established, with the dynastic disputes of the preceding century definitively over), proudly symbolising the unity of the English nation with all its values.[54] The second was the Church of England, which shared its supremacy widely by allowing other Christian religions to exist freely (the last legal restrictions on Unitarians and Catholics, for example, were lifted from 1813 to 1829). Finally, there was the United Grand Lodge of England, which had high-ranking aristo-

---

[54] In fact, it was during this period that the British monarchy obtained a founding legend, anchoring the royal symbols and pomp in an 'invented' tradition, as did Scotland at the same time—and Freemasonry in the preceding century! See David Cannadine, 'The Context, Performance and Meaning of Ritual: The British Monarchy and the "Invention of Tradition", c. 1820–1977', in *The Invention of Tradition*, eds. Eric Hobsbawm, and Terence Ranger (Cambridge: Cambridge University Press, 1983), 101–164.

crats of the kingdom for its dignitaries (starting with the Grand Master, who was Prince of Wales several times),[55] and whose Lodges united military men, bourgeois citizens, small traders and ecclesiastics under one banner. Each Lodge had a Chaplain from the orders of one of England's religions, but most frequently from the Anglican Church (as was very often the case for the Grand Chaplain of the UGLE itself).

However, following the 1813 union, the impressive rise of the UGLE was also the work of its first Grand Master, and probably the only one in its history to have exercised real personal power: Augustus Frederick, Duke of Sussex (1773–1843). During his 30 year as Grand Master, he presided over the profound re-shaping, but also the consolidation, of English Masonry. He gave it the security of a long mandate, which guaranteed the continuity of his work, as well as the prestige and authority of his rank. He was son of a king, brother of a king, and very close to Queen Victoria, as her favorite uncle!

Despotic, but clear sighted and respected, he was in particular responsible for the ritual unification of the symbolic degrees. This was possible thanks to the work of the Lodge of Reconciliation over which he ruled from 1813 to 1816, and also the work of that fundamental Order for the English, the 'Holy Royal Arch of Jerusalem', with the major reform of 1835. Thus, he steered English Masonry towards what is generally called its 'dechristianization'! However, we should not fall into the trap of thinking, as it is commonly done in France, that this was the start of

---

[55] In 1919, the UGLE even went so far as to add 'a border of eight golden leopards' faces' to its coat of arms. These were emblems of the British monarchy, and emphasized 'the long association of the Royal House with Freemasonry'.

secularization. English Masons would have been disgusted by such an idea. It was in fact a repositioning of the rituals and symbolic teachings of Masonry, on an exclusively Old Testament basis. Sussex, a Hebraist and collector of old Bibles, was also an ardent 'philosemite' and one of the first members of the 'Royal Blood' to visit the Great Synagogue of London, in 1809. However, this was more than just a personal choice, and the bases for it were not only moral, philosophical, or religious.

It was because English Masonry became non-denominational—meaning that it was not connected to any particular religion, at least in the Judeo-Christian universe—that it was able to set up Lodges all around the world. This particularly included Lodges in England's newly conquered territories: with the military barracks and colonial authorities, recruiting local nobles of very diverse religions into the Lodges of the empire played an important role in its sociological implantation among the peoples it incorporated. To be convinced of this, we only need to read the famous poem by Kipling (who was a talented and melancholic eulogist of British glory), *The Mother Lodge*:

> We'd Bola Nath, Accountant,
> An' Saul the Aden Jew,
> An' Din Mohammed, draughtsman
> Of the Survey Office too;
> There was Babu Chuckerbutty,
> An' Amir Singh the Sikh,
> An' Castro from the fittin'-sheds,
> The Roman Catholick!
>
> ...
>
> For monthly, after Labour,

We'd all sit down and smoke
(We dursn't give no banquets,
Lest a Brother's caste were broke),
An' man on man got talkin'
Religion an' the rest,
An' every man comparin'
Of the God 'e knew the best.

All (or almost all) the religions of the empire are represented here, and Kipling emphasises that God was not a cause for dispute and divisions between the brothers, but rather their common denominator in this atmosphere of tact and courtesy regarding religion, which led them not to drink or eat after labour; thus breaking with a well-established Masonic tradition!

In a statement in the *Times*, Kipling spoke again of this religious diversity:

> I was entered by a member of the Brahmo Samaj[56] (a Hindu), passed by a Mohammedan, and raised by an Englishman. Our Tyler was an Indian Jew.

This, in Kipling's eyes, as in those of most of his Brothers, was an essential marker of Freemasonry: being a peaceful confluence of all religions.

Kipling was entered in Lahore in 1886. What he tells us of his Mother Lodge goes back to this time: he was only an active member of it for two years. The connections

---

[56] The reference to the Brahmo Samaj is in itself interesting: this theist religious movement, founded in India in the 1830s, is inspired by elements taken from Hinduism, Islam, and Christianity. The Brahmo Samaj promotes meditation as the essence of spiritual life and accords great importance to social concerns such as philanthropic action, the abolition of the caste system, and the emancipation of women.

between French Freemasons and the Masonry of Kipling and his Brothers had been broken for around 10 years.

If we now collect together all the preceding data and compare it to the French situation and the climate at the time in French Lodges, it is easy to understand that neither Kipling nor any of the members of his Lodge could have accepted the 1877 decision, and that it could only be met with shock and unqualified rejection from English Masons. It was as if the French had announced that they would no longer maintain relationships with a monarchy (even a parliamentary one), or with a country which had an official church (even if it authorised others). It was as if they were saying that the queen of England was no longer respectable, because she had been crowned at Westminster, violating the 'liberty of conscience' of her subjects! For them, to question faith in God (seen in the English way—that is, far from any doctrinal controversy and generally considering a theological dispute as a perfectly out-of-place and idle exchange) was to question the whole British world, the throne, the empire and of course that highly respected social institution: Masonry. In England, as had once been the case in France, this Masonry, with its rituals and vows, had since time immemorial asked that each initiate take God as his witness and kiss the Bible to seal his commitment, in the Lodge as in many acts of public life.

In France, even today, this is often interpreted as an almost scandalous manifestation of 'dogmatic' intolerance, a view that Anglo-Saxon Masons simply could not understand! For them, it revealed an almost consensual and obvious intangible moral and social foundation that gave meaning not only to Freemasonry but also to the life in general. This was a deep conviction in a country that for almost two centuries, far from the disturbances on the Continent, had made religious and political peace based on great diversity the foundation for its prosperity and national pride.

Moreover, even if they had thought about it, the English would probably not have been able to envisage such a thing coming from the French Masons. In the eighteenth century, English and French Masonry were the same, apart from a few small details. Even in 1858, the rituals of the GODF promulgated under Grand Master Murat explicitly referred to a Supreme Being, easily identifiable with God.[57] Consequently, the English were not dreaming when they claimed that the two strains of Masonry shared common sources, and that for a very long time, almost forever, they had walked parallel Masonic paths. Was the history of rituals, which were so important in their eyes because they lay at the heart of Masonic life, not clear evidence of this?

Nevertheless, the GODF feigned dismay rather than joy at the English reaction. The French were apparently very surprised, but was this entirely sincere?

Even in 1884, the President of the Council of the Order of the GODF, Brother Charles Cousin, wrote to the Prince of Wales to plead the GODF's cause again. Deploring 'the ostracism suffered by French Masons', he uses the words that his predecessor, Antoine de Saint-Jean, used in 1877, denying that the GODF had wanted to 'profess atheism'. He emphasises that Frédéric Desmons (rapporteur for the contentious proposal) was a 'Protestant pastor' and

---

[57] The initiation ceremony concludes: 'May the Great Architect of the Universe help me'! To this, all the Brothers respond: "Amen." The training for the degree of Apprentice defines Freemasonry as having 'for its foundation the existence of God and the immortal soul'.

a member of the 'Reformed Church', perhaps expecting that these pious references, somewhat unexpected from his pen, might move his royal correspondent!

However, the response, delivered several weeks later by the Grand Secretary of England, drove the message home. The English dignitary stated that the Grand Lodge of England 'had never supposed' (English humour?) that in modifying its *Constitution* 'the Grand Orient wanted to formally profess atheism and materialism'. However, he immediately added that

> the Grand Lodge of England maintains and has always maintained that belief in God is the first great mark of any true and authentic Masonry, and that unless this belief is professed as the essential principle of its existence, no association can claim to inherit the traditions and practices of ancient and pure Masonry.[58]

This text must not only be read, but also considered and kept in mind. In it, the UGLE clearly expresses what it considers to be the unambiguous, essential foundation for Masonic philosophy and it does not mince its words. We should remember this when reading—in the *Basic Principles*, for example—the term 'Supreme Being', which in France often gave rise to idle comments and bizarre or complacent interpretations. The 1884 text clearly states that this term refers to God and God alone; however this God is envisaged, and the English all know about that!

---

[58] Adrien Juvanon, *Vers la lumière* (Paris: Imprimerie centrale de la bourse, 1926), 66 and after.

What Is to Be Done about the French?

However, from December 1877, the UGLE had decided to handle the practical consequences of this little tremour. The question could be expressed quite concisely: 'What should we do if French Brothers ask to be admitted as visitors to an English Lodge?'

As we have seen, until this point, everything was simple, with a visitor merely required to produce a Masonic document. Now, there was a need to distinguish between 'recognised' Brothers and the rest.

The interesting thing in this first UGLE attitude is the fact that it did not tar all GODF Brothers with the same brush, as one might say. It did not rule out that some Masons, or even entire Lodges of the Grand Orient, might have stayed faithful to traditional principles. After all, around a third of Lodges had not been in favour of the proposal!

Finally, in February 1878, the pragmatic and concrete English position ended.[59] The UGLE adopted a very simple procedure: it would admit any brother from France who could prove, with a document making this explicit, that he had been initiated into a Lodge that referred to the Great Architect. If no trustworthy person could testify in his favour, he was required to make a spontaneous oath of his personal faith in the Great Architect on the Bible![60]

It is worth noting here that, once again, this procedure (and we do not in truth know how many times it was used!) implicitly presumed that for every Brother in this

---

[59] See the text published in Oswald Wirth, *Qui est* régulier? (Paris: Editions du Symbolisme, 1938), 127.

[60] Michael Brodsky, 'The Regular Freemason: A Short History of Masonic Regularity', *AQC* 106 (1993): 112.

situation, the GAOTU necessarily referred to the Bible God of English ritual. This could be naivety, or a misunderstanding of the real situation on the Continent, particularly in France, which in the future and right up to the present day would be the cause of much ambiguity and some deceptions.

The official declaration made on this occasion by the UGLE in March 1878 marked an important historical step:

> The Grand Lodge, whilst always anxious to receive in the most fraternal spirit the Brethren of any foreign Grand Lodge whose proceedings are conducted according to the Ancient Landmarks of the Order, of which a belief in T.G.A.O.T.U. is the first and most important, cannot recognize as "true and genuine" Brethren any who have been initiated in lodges which either deny or ignore that belief."[61]

This was the first time that the notion of recognition was applied to other Grand Lodges and to international relations. It is important to remember that this had never been the case before.

It is also important to note (because this fact is often hidden) that in 1899 the young GLDF took steps to be recognised by London, having kept the GAOTU after much debate.

The Grand Secretary of the UGLE told the GLDF that such recognition was out of the question, particularly because the Lodges of the GLDF had not received their warrants from a Grand Lodge, but from a Supreme Council

---

[61] Robert Freke Gould, *The History of Freemasonry*, vol. 3 (London, 1886–1888): 26.

and because the presence of the Bible was not obligatory in these Lodges![62]

In this case, the UGLE was very swift, taking no more than three days to reply, but we should remember that Fachoda had only just happened.

This system survived, above all for France, which had justified the 1878 decision, until 1913, when the first 'regular' (because it was recognised as such) Obedience was created in France. Nevertheless, this new regularity, a sine qua non of recognition, needed to be made more specific and complete.

This would take almost half a century.

---

[62] Information from J. Hamill on the Philalethes mailing list, posted by Yosho Washizu (September 2, 2007).

Chapter 6

From the Creation of the GLNIR to the Basic Principles

Damned French

O nce again, in an ironic twist of fate, it was under pressure from the French that in 1913 the English were forced to take a new step.

Since 1877, little had happened in this area, except an event in 1905 that is somewhat forgotten today but relevant here.

In this year, the three Grand Lodges agreed that:

> The question of recognizing a new Grand Lodge in any Colony or other territory in which the three Grand Lodges [England, Scotland, and Ireland] have equal jurisdiction and have Warranted Lodges working therein, shall not be taken into consideration unless at least two-thirds of the Lodges under each jurisdiction or such other proportion as the three Grand Lodges shall agree in the light of local circumstances have signified their adhesion to such new body; and such recognition shall only be granted by agreement of the three Grand Lodges.[63]

We can see that the procedure of 'recognition' (this time the word is clearly stipulated) began with a colonial prob-

---

[63] James Daniel, 'UGLE's External Relations 1950–2000: Policy and Practice', *AQC* 117 (2004): 2.

lem (which in this instance first concerned Queensland, in Australia).

It is remarkable that in this initial approach, it was never a matter of purely Masonic, philosophical or religious considerations: we were talking about English, Scottish or Irish Lodges 'across the seas', so this question never arose. Still, the problem of the conditions for recognition of a now independent Grand Lodge was beginning to emerge.

However, the formulation of the rules of recognition, ambiguously embracing the notion of regularity (because this became the necessary but not sufficient sine qua non of recognition), did not surface until a little later—only recently, in 1929.[64]

It was between these two events that the Grande Loge nationale indépendante et régulière (GLNIR: Regular and Independent National Grand Lodge) was created in France, for France and the French colonies.

Paradoxically, this was a gift from the Grand Orient to the UGLE, allowing it to enter the French Masonic scene! It was done out of 'secular' intolerance on the part of the Grand Orient, which is easy to understand when taken in its historical context, but which today we can judge impartially as abusive, unfair and above all ill advised.

Three Brothers, including Edouard de Ribaucourt, who would become first Grand Master of the GLNIR, had been 'armed' as Knights Beneficent of the Holy City, in Geneva in 1910. The other two were Camille Savoire and Guillaume Bastard. Reviving the Centre des Amis, a Lodge that had been dormant since the start of the nineteenth century, they wanted to work there according to

---

[64] A first version had been envisaged from 1920, just after the First World War. Daniel, 'UGLE's External Relations', 3.

the Rectified Scottish Rite, which they actually understood very poorly, and with the sole purpose (as Savoire
put it in 1935) of

> creating a Masonic hotbed that escapes any
> political influence, strictly kept apart from dis-
> cussions concerning political parties and social
> clans and the controversies on burning ques-
> tions that concern them or relate to religious
> or metaphysical scandals, and above all to the
> selfish claims of corporatist or social-class in-
> terests.[65]

Confronted with the secular intransigence of the leaders of the Grand Orient, they accepted a rewriting of the
rituals, and particularly of the prayers, which became
'invocations'. This almost entirely deprived them of their
initial religious nature, proper to this Christian Rite. Despite this, in a last-minute maneuver, they were blocked
by the GODF convent in 1913. A few days later, they
decided to call upon England to obtain recognition for
a new Obedience formed from two Lodges that had left
the GODF.[66]

The affair, personally followed by Lord Ampthill, then
Pro Grand Master (executive Grand Master) of the
UGLE, was over in a few weeks. Ribaucourt actively
brainwashed the English a little and made them believe
that many Lodges would follow him. He mentioned at

---

[65] Camille Savoire, *Pourquoi voulons-nous réveiller le Rite rectifié en
France?* (1935). Incidentally, this tells us much about the atmosphere in the Lodges of the GODF at the time.

[66] This was when the Anglaise of Bordeaux joined with the Centre
des Amis. There is an excellent analysis on this subject in Pierre
Noël, 'Heurs et malheurs du Rite Ecossais Rectifié en France au
XXème siècle', http://www.ordo-ab-chao.org/ordo/Doc/heurs.
pdf (accessed February 26, 2015).

least a dozen Lodges ready to join the breakaways. Still, he put forward three key arguments to support the request for English recognition: the fact that the ritual of the Rectified Scottish Rite had been used at the initiation of the Duke of Kent in 1790 (!); that all the proceedings were placed 'under the aegis of the Great Architect of the Universe', the Bible being open at the prologue to the Gospel of John; and that religious and political controversies would be forbidden.

No reference was made here to the *Basic Principles*, which had not yet been promulgated, but we can see that the key points had been addressed. Looking at it from London, it could easily appear that the wind of revolt hoped for in 1877 had just risen and that the GODF was going to return to the bosom of 'pure and ancient' Masonry. English recognition was obtained on December 3, 1913, on the assurance received by the Duke of Connaught, Grand Master, that the new Obedience was committing 'to adhere to the principles of Freemasonry that we consider fundamental and essential'.

We must suppose that these principles were those mentioned in Ribaucourt's letter, cited above.

We know that the GLNIR remained confidential for a long time and was above all populated by Englishmen living in France and practicing Masonry in their language. Oswald Wirth, a highly influential Freemason at this time, cruelly enjoyed calling it 'the English Grand Lodge of France'. Moreover, while corresponding mainly by mail and at a distance, there had been no attempt to check what these founding Brothers meant by 'GAOTU'. Although some of them were not afraid of a vaguely deist symbology, the much more religious view of the English was undoubtedly not their cup of tea! In the rather stormy debate at the GODF convent, before the final split, Ribaucourt (reproached for maintaining the GAO-TU) had even declared, revealingly, that 'it is a symbol'! He did not think it necessary to express this view in his letters to Lord Ampthill!

Moreover, it is significant that once the war was over, Edouard de Ribaucourt resigned from his post, which did not mean that he had given up Masonry. In fact, in 1935, he attended the founding of the Grand Prieuré des Gaules (Grand Priory of the Gauls) with his friend Camille Savoire,[67] who would soon resign from the GODF after 12 year as Grand Commander of its Grand College of the Rites, the organization presiding over the high degrees of the Grand Orient.

Formulating Principles

However, what interests us here is the fact that the UGLE 'came out of the woods' and this time very officially gave proper recognition in France (for the first time), and more generally to a major country which was in no way part of the British Empire.

This clearly led France to improvise somewhat, in an effort not to miss this chance. Nevertheless, from 1920, sensing that the incident was bound to be repeated, the UGLE finally thought to formulate the principles for recognition more precisely. As we know, the results of this

---

[67] Who in the 1935 texts cited above would specify when knighted in Geneva that, as a 'free thinker', he was not put off by the (according to him very pared down) Christianity of the Order, and that the Gospel of Saint John did not seem to him to be a 'religious book' but a 'very eclectic summary of ancient esotericism'.

work came in 1929.

This was a very specific period in the history of the British Empire. It marked the start of the destabilising, the crumbling, and then, barely 15 years later, the disintegration of this empire, which London attempted to recuperate in the form of the Commonwealth. Just as his majesty's government fought to find ways of preserving its future influence over countries drawn to the 'open sea' and the taste for independence, the English Masonic authorities, which had established Lodges and districts directly attached to London all around the empire, sought a way of formulating the rules that would allow these Lodges (and the future independent Grand Lodges that would inevitably result) to maintain a connection with the Mother Grand Lodge of the World. In return for their accepting this honorary status for the United Grand Lodge of England, these new Grand Lodges would be 'recognised'.

Naturally, applying these rules created no real difficulties for the Grand Lodges around the world, which were born of the old 'single system' of the English Grand Lodge. Raised on the English principles, and mostly sharing the country's culture, the new Masonic powers (such as India or South Africa) would see no difficulties in the formulation of these principles, which for them were virtually self-evident. These principles brought no innovation and nothing problematic, aside from sometimes convoluted wording.

Instead, the problem came from the need that rapidly became clear to extend them to Grand Lodges that had always been independent but had begun more or less avidly to seek recognition from London, often to boost their legitimacy.

Basically, this was the case illustrated by the GLNIR from 1913, when it got the London Masonic authorities to intervene in France, even though they were not seeking do so! While remaining the smallest and most precarious of the French Obediences, the GLNIR succeeded in becoming the only one to enjoy the support of the most powerful Grand Lodge in the world!

'Pure Masonry' According to Oswald Wirth

However, before we come to the implementation, particularly after the Second World War, of this system of *Basic Principles* (an implementation that was not as simple as it appeared), we need to briefly examine a prewar French reaction.

For the first time, a 'great witness' of Masonry in France was addressing the question of regularity, bringing the French vision face to face with the recent English definition, henceforth applied in France in at least one Obedience. The work he published then is undoubtedly the source of a certain number of confusions and ambiguities surrounding regularity, which are still present in France today. That writer was Oswald Wirth.

Wirth's work, still highly valued in France, has on the whole aged badly. For a long time, his passion for tarot and 'curative' magnetism, his approximate alchemy, and his rudimentary Kabbalah greatly contributed to obscuring the question of Masonic symbolism in France. At least, however, at a time when hardly anyone in the French Lodges paid attention to ritual details (at least in the GLDF and the GODF), he had the merit of drawing everyone's attention to the fact that this was where the fundamentals of Masonry could be found.[68] But Oswald Wirth had another quality: he looked at Masonic universalism and stayed informed about international evolutions.

The book that he published in 1938 is entitled *Qui est régulier? (Who Is Regular?)*. This 150-page volume is actually an artificial collection of 25 articles that had already been published between 1913 and 1936 in the journal that he ran, entitled *Le Symbolisme*. They make up a string of chapters, sometimes with rather unclear transitions, which constantly return to the same themes.

In fact, on the title page, Wirth's subtitle expresses his vision of regularity: 'Pure Masonism under the regime of the Grand Lodges inaugurated in 1717'. The work therefore addresses the question of what 'pure Masonism' really is. It was, in any case, a pure neologism.

The editor of *Le Symbolisme* could have revisited the purely administrative sense of the word in France and England throughout the eighteenth and during the nineteenth century. Instead, he chose another approach, since 1877 had occurred and the *Basic Principles* had been published around a decade earlier. This is expressed in the principal thesis of his little book.

Wirth's key argument is that 'pure Masonism' was codified by Anderson in 1723, in General Head I of the *Charges* in his *Constitutions*.[69] He interprets this text as immediately

---

[68] Which did not prevent Wirth, who was Venerable Master at the Travail et vrais amis fidèles Lodge of the GLDF, from spending his time studying purely societal or even political subjects with Brothers from his Lodge. See René Désaguliers, 'A propos de René Guénon: Points d'histoire maçonnique', *Renaissance Traditionnelle* 41 (1980): 29–32.

[69] It is rather striking and even quite funny to note that today certain Masonic circles for which Wirth was a hero in his time now

instituting in young London Masonry a total 'liberty of conscience' in the belated and narrowly French sense of the term (although Wirth pretends not to realise this). He even rages against the 1738 version, which he claims betrayed 'pure Masonism' by introducing God into the heart of the Lodge.

I will not dwell here on the reasons why this reading, which after him became tradition in France, is in fact profoundly flawed. It nevertheless started a line of defense that has been adopted by many French Masonic figures after him, and notably by Joannis Corneloup, who was Grand Commander *ad vitam* of the GODF's Grand Collège des Rites. This theory states that regularity means following Anderson's 1723 text, provided that it is interpreted as outlined above. It asserts that the UGLE, 'only' founded in 1813 by two Grand Lodges that for 60 years accused each other of irregularity, merely embedded the 'schism' (in Wirth's words) introduced into Masonic thinking by the 1738 version.

I wish to re-emphasise that this vision has little support from English scholars;[70] British Masons see the succession of versions of the *Constitutions* as a regular progression towards the 1815[71] synthesis. This synthesis was accepted without difficulty by the gathered members of the two Grand Lodges, which had undoubtedly disagreed in

---

assert that true Masonry (theirs, of course, which they call 'pure Masonism') came 'pre-Anderson', and that they consider Anderson a dangerous revisionist.

[70] See in particular the excellent article by Eric Ward, 'Anderson's Freemasonry not Deistic', *AQC* 80 (1967): 36–57. Following the contribution, a comment from a young French correspondent attempting criticism called upon Corneloup. One can imagine the effect that this to say the least incongruous and undoubtedly falsely naive reference must have had on Eric Ward.

[71] Date of publication of the UGLE's first *Book of Constitutions*.

the past, but not on these points!

In addition to this, the sometimes rather frivolous French authors (among others) who comment on this evolution generally fail to mention (because they simply do not know) that in two intermediary versions of the *Constitutions*, published in the latter half of the eighteenth century,[72] it was the 1723 text that was used!

Oswald Wirth was one of the few Masons of his time who took any interest in the very foundations of Freemasonry, and just for this he deserves our respect. Reading his elegant classical prose, we can see how deep the cultural divide between French Masonry and English Masonry had already become, leaving room for all kinds of misunderstandings.

---

[72] In 1756 and 1784.

CHAPTER 7

STANDARDS AND PRACTICES FOR ANGLO-SAXON REGULARITY AND FOR RECOGNITION BY LONDON— AND ITS FRIENDS

Managing the System

From the 1950s in particular (if we allow for the inevitable interruption by the war), the UGLE needed little convincing to join the game of international recognitions. It had found a way of extending and even institutionalising its honorary privilege in the global Masonic community—the very privilege that the Grand Orient de France had refused it in 1775, for reasons unrelated to any metaphysical debate. However, this is where the clash of cultures started to become apparent.

There is not sufficient space here for me to go over the list of incidents that have peppered the world of Anglo-Saxon regularity, especially from the 1970s. Although many Grand Lodges were recognised, others were 'derecognised' for various reasons, almost always related to the question of the Volume of Sacred Law and the affirmation of faith in God, Great Architect of the Universe. This was the case in Belgium in 1979, leading to the de-recognition of the Grande Loge de Belgique and the subsequent creation of the Grande Loge régulière de Belgique (Regular Grand Lodge of Belgium), which has not altered its doctrine since. The question of 'irregular' inter-visiting (the other criteria having been left unquestioned) also played a role in these incidents with the UGLE, but less than is generally believed: the Swiss Grand Lodge Alpina was implicated and for this reason relationships with London were suspended between 12 and 15 months in 1965 and 1971. Every time, Alpina insisted that it would not happen again (was this so certain?), and recognition was reestablished![73] The UGLE, which rectified its position in a few months in both cases, noted on this occasion that several European regular Grand Lodges had not followed it in its initial action of de-recognition. This clearly implies that certain principles were more fundamental than others.

A close examination of the 1929 *Principles* shows that some points in this text are closely connected to English Masonic culture and are only strictly applicable to Masonic traditions directly attached to this culture.

Let us take a simple (if slightly technical) example that often goes unnoticed but that is in fact very telling. Point 3 of the 1929 text requires that the 'Three Great Lights of Freemasonry' (the Compasses, the Square, and the Volume of Sacred Law) should be exhibited and used for the oath. However, we should remember that this requirement belongs to the tradition of the Antients. This tradition essentially triumphed when the union took place in 1813. In all the Masonic traditions belonging to the Moderns (the oldest, we must remember!), the 'Three Great Lights' do exist (the three 'objects' are present), but not under this name, or in this arrangement. Among the Moderns throughout the eighteenth century in England

---

[73] Nevertheless, Alpina reoffended several times, particularly in 1991. The controversial intervisiting mainly concerned the Grande Loge de France, to which Alpina apparently had a long-term attachment. In light of these incidents, it is easier to understand the role still played even recently by the Swiss Obedience in the Basel Affair. In 1990, for the same reason, the English Brothers were asked not to visit German Lodges anymore, even though these were recognized under the aegis of the United Grand Lodges of Germany.

and everywhere in France, and continuing throughout the nineteenth century in France, only the Worshipful Master's Sword was placed on the Bible (or Gospel). In the French Modern Rite (at least in its original, 'traditional' form), the Compasses are placed on the Worshipful Master's altar and the Square on the cushion used for the oath. In the Rectified Scottish Rite (a 'Modern' Rite), the Compasses and the Square are constantly intertwined and placed on the Worshipful Master's altar, but away from the Bible. Again, only the sword is placed on the Bible.

In short, to fulfill all the requirements of the *Basic Principles*, it is necessary to be English or to practice the English Rite![74]

Here, as elsewhere, 'reasonable adjustments' and a certain freedom of interpretation are therefore required. The English tacitly admitted this: the way of arranging columns, chandeliers, compasses or square is seen as a secondary concern. Although there are eight principles in the 1929 declaration, the most important of these relate to the Supreme Being and the Volume of Sacred Law.

The Contemporary Situation

The Anglo-Saxon system of regularity has nevertheless

---

[74] The rituals of the Ancient and Accepted Scottish Rite for the blue degrees, only written in France in 1804 (*Guide des Maçons Ecossais* in their latest printed version), completely satisfy the formal criteria, because they are essentially based precisely on a translation of the ritual of the Antients. Nevertheless, they contain important basic characteristics that later disappeared, particularly (to cite just one key point) the fact that in the first ritual of the French Ancient and Accepted Scottish Rite, the Lodge is opened 'in the Name of God and St. John of Scotland'. This is very different from the current wording of this ritual in the GLDF, for example.

suffered several attacks over recent years.

The first, which is little discussed despite being very significant, concerns the principle of 'exclusive territorial jurisdiction', which stipulates that there can only be one regular Grand Lodge per country. This features absolutely nowhere in the *Basic Principles*. It is a practice inherited from American customs, which during the nineteenth century for reasons of civil peace within a young nation stipulated that there could only be one Grand Lodge for each of the states in the Union. Nevertheless, little by little, or in any case tacitly, England came to apply this principle.

However, the morally untenable situation created by the duality of 'Caucasian' (that is, 'white') Grand Lodges and Grand Lodges of Prince Hall ('black' Grand Lodges) in the United States forced England to stop hiding behind this principle and finally recognise two Grand Lodges per state in the United States in the 1990s! It is also worth mentioning the special case of Germany. After the war, the country picked up the scattered pieces of a troubled Masonic history to form a Confederation of United Grand Lodges of Germany, all united under one theoretical umbrella, which was the only one recognized by London.

The system of international regularity is therefore not a monolith. It is in fact a contradictory universe in which Obediences that are recognised and unrecognised by London share the same theoretical space. We will examine this later. Consequently, many combinations are possible, at least in theory and to a certain point. There are of course insurmountable landmarks.

In fact, I have not yet discussed this indefinable word

'landmark'! Although it is already present in Anderson,[75] representing the eighth and final point of the *Basic Principles* ('That the principles of the Antient Landmarks, customs and usages of the Craft shall be strictly observed'.), it always remains completely enigmatic. Its etymological meaning is clear: 'milestone, limit'. In short, it refers to the 'yellow lines' (in modern language) that should not be crossed, but an exhaustive list of these has never been provided. Many authors, particularly the American Mackey, author of the *Encylopaedia of Freemasonry* (1874), have tried to draw up an impressive and highly debatable catalog of these landmarks. Mackey lists twenty-five! However, there is nothing consensual or very convincing.

On the rare occasions when an official text gives an explanation, it only ever concerns two points. As the Count of Scarborough put it unambiguously at a Grand Lodge meeting in 1952, when he was Grand Master of the UGLE:

> We require each of our members to believe in God, and our references are based on the Volume of Sacred Law. They are our essential *Landmarks*.

This is closely comparable to the third and final 'criterion' for recognition according to the American Grand Lodges: 'Adherence to the Ancient Landmarks'. This would tell us little if the text did not go on to explain: 'Specifically, a Belief in God, the Volume of the Sacred Law as an indispensable part of the lodge'.

---

[75] More precisely, in the *General Regulations* (article XXIX), published in 1723 *Constitutions* (page 70) and penned by George Payne, Grand Master in 1720, we read: 'Provided always that the *Old Landmarks* be carefully preserved'. However, no explanation is provided for this statement.

The American Example

This last reference brings us to the case of America, which I will address briefly here.

During 2012–2014, in a troubled French Masonic landscape, it was common to evoke what might jokingly be called 'the American martingale'. In short, the idea was that the English, entrenched in their cold dogmatism, could never accept the underlying regularity of the French Obediences, which was much too difficult for them to decrypt. Consequently, they still refused to recognise these Obediences, while the Americans, more open and more 'modern', would readily consent. In a way, you had to get around London via Baltimore.

In support of this brilliant intuition, the fact was cited that in the pre-war period, many American Grand Lodges had already recognised the GLDF. This was completely true, but a little reductive. Closer examination yields interesting discoveries.

In around 1920, just fewer than 25 American Grand Lodges recognised the Grande Loge de France.[76] However, two key points should be emphasised:

- The first is that all these recognitions had been obtained between 1917 and 1919, or during the period when, following the Great War, America had in a way 're-discovered' France. Without a doubt, this was one of the effects of this slightly nostalgic and sentimental return to the early days of the American Republic ('Lafayette, here we are!'), in the context of a renewed fraternity

---

[76] See Paul Bessel, 'U.S. Recognition of French Grand Lodges in the 1900s', *Heredom: The Transactions of the Scottish Rite Research Society* 5 (1996): 221–244.

of arms that took the Americans back to their
founding myths. In the glow of common victo-
ry, American Masons had spontaneously recon-
nected with the French.

• This is so true (and this is the second significant
fact) that during the same period, as is often
forgotten, around half of the same American
Grand Lodges also recognised the Grand Orient de France! That is to say that the atmosphere
of enthusiasm undoubtedly played a large role
in these recognitions.

All the same, in around 1960, around 20 American Grand
Lodges still recognised the GLDF.[77]

In September 1953, the Grande Loge de France decided
to reinstate the mandatory presence of the Bible on the
altar in all its Lodges. This serves as a reminder that it had
long disappeared from most of them. In 1955, it adopted
a Declaration of Principles, which in reality was almost an
exact copy of a recent Swiss text.[78] This document asserted two essential points: the fact that the GLDF conduct-
ed its entire works 'to the Glory of the Great Architect
of the Universe'; and the presence of the Bible in Lodges.

In the wake of this, still in 1955, a great maneuver began: the project for a Grand United Lodge of France,
which was to bring together the GLDF, the GLNF, and
the GODF. Evidently, it failed. The complex and shifting
relationships between the GODF and the GLDF, a true
soap opera of Masonic history in France for over a centu-

---

[77] See Paul Bessel, 'U.S. Grand Lodges' Withdrawal of Recognition
of the GLF in the 1950s and 1960s', http://bessel.org/masrec/glf-
derec.htm (accessed August 10, 2015).

[78] Text adopted at the Assembly of Delegates of the Swiss Grand
Lodge Alpina, on May 21, 1949, in Winterthur.

ry, led to a crisis in 1965 with the rupture of the SCDF into two factions, and with certain Brothers leaving the GLDF for the GLNF.

It is very interesting to examine what the American Grand Lodges thought of the French Masonic situation in this period and how they judged it. The COGMINA annual reports are a useful guide here.

1960 (page 53):

> The Grand Lodge of France has suspended relations with the Grand Orient of France by action taken against the last Annual Communication of the Grand Lodge of France.[79] However, the Grand Master of the Grand Lodge of France advises that some inter-visitation continues despite the action of his Grand Lodge.

1963 (pages 43–44):

> The Officers of the Grande Loge Nationale insist that intervisitation continues between the Lodges of the Grand Lodge of France and the Grand Orient. They present indisputable proof of this as something that goes on in the Paris area as well as in the Provinces. The Grand Lodge of France has little hope of being considered regular as long as fraternal relations are continued with the Grand Orient of France.

1964 (page 48):

> It seems to be difficult for the Grand Lodge of France to sever relations completely with the Grand Orient of France. All of our information indicates that intervisitation continues.

---

[79] In September 1959.

We can firstly see that the observations only ever concern controversial inter-visits with this 'damned' GODF, irregular due to its 'guilty' renunciation of 1877.

But above all, in 1965, this time bitterly lamenting the treaty of alliance that had again been concluded between the la GLDF and the GODF in September 1964, making any recognition impossible, the conference looked back on the progress that, in its eyes, the GLDF had accomplished in spite of this in recent years. Here, we can read an astonishing statement (pages 39–40):

> Some years ago, the Grand Lodge of France voted to *make mandatory a belief in God* (!), and the display of the Volume of the Sacred Law.

This allows us to understand what happened: a perfect and gigantic misunderstanding.

At the start of the 1960s—and a fortiori already in around 1920!—what was France in the eyes of an average Mason from Minnesota or South Dakota? Would he even have been able to pinpoint it correctly on a world map? How many Americans were living in Paris then? Certainly not masses of them. At the time, it was a long boat trip to Europe, and we certainly were not yet in the 'information society' or the 'global village' where we live today. In other words, to evaluate the regularity of Grand Lodges in France, American Masons simply read the documents sent to them, with no further comment or explanation of their context. These undoubtedly included the famous 1955 *Declaration of Principles*, which had in fact been designed more for Masons outside of France than for those in the country!

Reading this text, there is no doubt that for them 'the

Glory of the Great Architect of the Universe' meant nothing more than 'the mandatory belief in God', especially if we add the presence of the Bible to this! For Anglo-Saxon Masons, who were perfectly unaware of the subtle French speculation about this 'vocabulary', it was self-evident that the GAOTU had never been anything other than a Masonic moniker for God. Obviously, the French Masonic situation, including in the GLDF, was in fact infinitely more complex.[80]

However, we can also understand that during this entire period, the American Grand Lodges that did not yet recognise the GLDF (that is, the vast majority of them) undoubtedly emphasised what they considered to be the only remaining problem: 'irregular' inter-visiting with the GODF. Up until recently, it was said in France that this was still the only matter needing to be dealt with to obtain precious American recognition.

This astonishing mix-up, which, we will see, had heavy consequences, undoubtedly continued up until 2003, when the famous Minnesota episode put an indisputable end to it.

Without repeating the details of this affair, we should remember that after temporarily obtaining its official recognition from the Grand Lodge of Minnesota (which was then forced to go back on its decision), the GLDF came before the commission to have its case examined in view of a recommendation for recognition that this commission could have addressed to the Grand Lodges

---

[80] In 2007, in Manchester, before an audience of English Masons, I sought to explain the many possible faces of the French Masonic situation in this domain: 'The Great Architect of the Universe in the French Masonic Tradition: Historical Problems and Misunderstandings', http://c5596214.myzen.co.uk/wordpress/wp-content/uploads/2013/02/GAOTU-France-Dachez2007.pdf.

of North America. I simply wish to reproduce here a few excerpts from the proceedings of the commission on this occasion:

> The Conference of Grand Masters of Masons of North America and the Conference of Grand Secretaries took place from February 16 to February 18, 2003, in Minneapolis, Minnesota ...
>
> 26 ... The Grand Chancellor of the GLDF, the Grand Chancellor of the GLF had asked for permission to speak to the commission two days earlier, and that he had said that the GLF requires all candidates to express a belief in a Supreme Being, that all GLF lodges are required to have the Bible open on their altars.

It is clear that the Grand Chancellor's announcement, skillfully playing on the ambiguity[81] (at least in the mouth of a Frenchman!) of the term 'Supreme Being', was trying to retain that same vagueness that had misled the Americans for so long. Basically, there was a desire to stick to the erroneous reading of the 1955 *Declaration of Principles*.

However, what follows is telling:

> 24. On Tuesday, February 18, the chairman and members of the Commission on Information for Recognition were introduced at the full session of the Conference of Grand Masters of Masons in North America, and the chairman presented the report .
>
> 27. The commission chairman then reported that the Deputy Grand Master of the GLF,

---

[81] Provided that his words were faithfully reported in the accounts of the commission.

who was at the Conference and who had attended the public session of the Commission on Sunday, later asked to speak to the commission. He told the commission members that he came to rectify untruths that had been made by the Grand Chancellor to the commission, and he apologized for the false information that had been given to the commission. He said he was speaking on behalf of the Grand Master of the GLF, and a telephone call was arranged with the GLF Grand Master in which he supported what the Deputy Grand Master was telling the commission now.

28. It was reported that the Deputy Grand Master of the GLF, and its Grand Master too, said that the GLF does not require all candidates to express a belief in a Supreme Being but instead leaves this entirely up to the conscience of each candidate, that the GLF considers continued intervisitations with the GOF to be essential, that the GLF does not want to talk with north american grand lodges about regularity and recognition but only social contacts, and that the GLF Grand Master will sent a letter to the commission with honest information.

We can imagine the effect that this complete volte-face must have had on the American Masonic dignitaries, especially given what lying represents in American culture. Their eyes must have virtually burst out of their sockets in the face of the true meaning (masked by an ambiguous vocabulary) of the 1955 *Declaration of Principles*.

Moreover, the following paragraph (the last in the account) is an eloquent expression of this laconicism:

> 29. It was reported in this public session that this was a great moment, and it brought closure to the entire issue of the GLF. This entire subject is now concluded.

Consequently, a recent assertion by a French Grand Master of a young Obedience (undoubtedly sincere but forced to manage a difficult dialogue) that the conception of God by American Masons was evidently more 'open' (?) than that of the English, and that it therefore gave a glimpse of a more tolerant and undoubtedly more inclusive understanding of regularity, aside from showing a very serious misunderstanding on his part of the religious culture of the United States, above all revealed a worrying amnesia concerning an event that took place only about a decade ago, and of which the conclusion was unequivocal.

Still, contact and collaboration between Masons on either side of the Atlantic is not impossible in all Obediences—quite the opposite. And the most fruitful works are sometimes the product of the most improbable meetings: Alain Bauer bears witness to this. My friend Alain de Keghel, former Grand Commander of the Supreme Council, Grand College of the Ancient and Accepted Scottish Rite of the GODF, and great connoisseur of American Masonry, also knows something of the matter.[82]

Although the world of Masonic regularity in Anglo-Saxon Obediences is undoubtedly sometimes a little contradictory, it is at least determined to manage its contradictions itself.

---

[82] Alain de Keghel, *Le Défi maçonnique américain* (Paris: Dervy, 2015).

An Arithmetic Regularity!

The global community of the regular Grand Lodges also has a sort of 'legal showcase': the World Conference of Masonic Regular Grand Lodges.

Created in 1995 in Mexico under the name 'World Conference of Grand Masters', it has met on average every 18 month since then, and 13 times in all. The most recent meeting was in Bucharest in 2014, and the next will take place in San Francisco in November 2015. It aims to envisage all the problems related to the development of (regular) Masonry in the world, without creating restrictive commitments through any decisions by the participating Grand Lodges.

From an initial 37 Grand Lodges, the number of participants reached 106 in 2014. These include representatives of regular Grand Lodges that are not necessarily recognised by the UGLE (even though the body recognizes just under 200!), or that may no longer be recognised. To be admitted to this conference, a Grand Lodge simply needs to be recognised by at least 50 Grand Lodges that are already members. In some ways, this is an arithmetic definition of regularity!

Naturally, although the recognition is not complete among the participants, for various reasons, the Masonic principles that the UGLE would call 'essential' are not meant to be questioned, and remain the same. Since the 1996 meeting in Estoril, point 4 of a common declaration has carefully emphasised that

> the Grand Masters understood that the main Masonic landmark: The belief in the Supreme Being, God and Grand Architect of the World

was the basic principle that united and oriented the entire Masonic work worldwide, towards peace, harmony, fraternity, tolerance and solidarity, with absolutely no interference on politics or religion.[83]

Nevertheless, certain French Masons who sometimes wonder what 'English' Masons might talk about when they are apparently so set on 'dogmatic' principles might be surprised by the themes tackled during the various conference round tables. For example, in 2014 in Bucharest topics included 'Freemasonry as a Social Commitment. How the Values of the Craft Can Change a Mason's Life and How a Mason Can Change the Society' (!) and 'Freemasonry and the Challenges of the Media. The Manner in Which We Communicate. What We Communicate. Adapting to the New Reality of Electronic Media.'[84]

Of course, it is very likely that these issues will never be discussed in the Lodges to which the members of this conference belong, as in their eyes, this is not their purpose. However, we can see that the world of regular Masonry is much more complex than we tend to think.

---

[83] World Conference of Regular Masonic Grand Lodges, 'II. Conference, Estoril and Cascaus, Portugal, 1996', http://wcrmgl.org/history/en/conference-estoril-and-cascais-1996.html (accessed February 26, 2015).

[84] National Grand Lodge of Romania, 'The 13th World Conference of Regular Masonic Grand Lodges', http://www.mlnr.ro/index.php/conferinta-mondiala/engleza/the-13th-world-conference-of-regular-masonic-grand-lodges (accessed February 25, 2015).

CHAPTER 8

THE FRENCH AVATARS OF REGULARITY SINCE 1945

Try, Try Again

In France, the question of Masonic unity, which has been asked since the Liberation, has often overlapped with that of the 'return' to regularity.

Several times—in 1955, 1965, 1974, 1986, 1995 and 2003—rather similar scenarios have been repeated. They have always had the same predictable and almost planned outcome after a few months—before the Basel saga, which lasted two years.

The two most significant attempts were those of 1955 and 1965, although the consequences were very different.

In all cases, the only (or almost the only) net result of the operations was a return to the starting point for the GLDF and the movement of Brothers towards the GLNF. Over time, the GLNF has even simplified its procedures. Long ago, it required 'irregular' Masons wishing to join it to be re-initiated: this was a 'remaking' like that seen in England in the eighteenth century![85] Later, it was generally satisfied with a vow and the payment of a chancery fee.

Every time, the same double difficulty arose: the Grand Orient, unable to give up its resolute orientation towards 'absolute liberty of conscience'[86] and its 'societal' con-

---

[85] This can still be seen in British Grand Lodges, such as England and Scotland.

[86] Meaning, in the French language, the refusal of any 'dogmatic affirmation', in the name of strict 'secularity'. To put it clearly, it refers to

cerns, never stayed with these attempts for long, or stayed out of them entirely. Meanwhile, the GLDF 'clung on' as often as possible, even to the point of suffering a rift, as in 1965. However, it too was always forced to give up, because imposing the English understanding of the GAO-TU on French Brothers of the GLDF and making them refuse temple entrance to Brothers from several other French Obediences (starting with the historical ones: the GODF and the Droit Humain) always turned out to be culturally untenable for the vast majority.

On several occasions, people have thought it possible to deny this historical and quite simply human situation, to force fate and change minds, if necessary using maneuvers by the convent, or often by dissimulation of inconvenient truths and half lies. Eventually, however, they had to face the truth: they were forced to either surrender or break away, which was necessarily a very minority and ultimately inglorious affair.

However, there were other issues, in particular the imperial ideology and self-perception of the Ancient and Accepted Scottish Rite (especially in the GLDF's version). These aspects are well worth developing in depth but go beyond the scope of this study.

I will therefore focus on the subject at hand, returning to the heart of the matter: Why is regularity in France a recurrent issue and such a problematic subject?

It is possible at least to give elements of an answer.

---

the refusal to speak of a Supreme Being in whatever form as a possible reference of any importance for Masonry, and even the refusal to make just mentioning the GAOTU mandatory, including if this reference is interpreted (as it is by most French Masons) as a 'pure symbol'.

From Caricature to Comprehension

The basic problem is that the image that French Masons have of Anglo-Saxon Masonry and its regularity (whether they call themselves 'regular' or not!) is a real caricature. I think I have shown that, before being the history of an idea, the history of regularity is that of an ambiguity, a deep misunderstanding.

According to this misunderstanding, on the one side, there are the 'English' and those who follow their banner. They defend a 'deist' or 'dogmatic' understanding of Freemasonry (certain French Masonic dignitaries would even say a 'mystic' understanding!), which imposes a belief in God as 'the Foundation and Cape-stone, the Cement and Glory of this ancient Fraternity' (in the words of Anderson, who actually only applied them to fraternal love).[87]

On the other side, supposedly, is a classic French Masonry, or at least a continental Masonry that dominates on the French side of the Channel. This is liberal, progressive and 'adogmatic' in nature. It is deeply attached to 'absolute' liberty of conscience—and even to the origin of this magnificent concept—and proudly opposed to the dogmatism of the English.

On one side, spiritualist imperialism, on the other, philosophical freedom: it looks like a simple choice, with its outcome already inscribed in the very terms used to present it. Unfortunately, it is actually a labourious caricature that shows a lack of knowledge or a poor understanding concerning the rise of a certain vision of Masonry. In Great Britain, this vision was constructed over at least two centuries. Above all, it did not differ tangibly over this period from the vision that prevailed in France.

---

[87] Anderson, *Constitutions*, 56.

At this point, we should remember an elementary truth that is easily established by documented history: from the start of the eighteenth century to the mid-nineteenth century, aside from a few local particularities related to the culture of populations and their way of expressing certain things, Freemasonry shared the same spirit and practically the same rituals on both sides of the Channel (or, as the British insist on calling it, the 'English' or 'British' Channel). Comparing the two, as with comparing two essentially irreconcilable worlds, is therefore illusory and, quite simply, a mistake. Moreover, although the expression 'liberty of conscience' did appear fairly early in the Masonic vocabulary, this did not happen in France, where the notion only took on a Masonic connotation very belatedly in the nineteenth century. The first time that it is mentioned in a Masonic text is (as stated above) in the 1738 edition (and not the 1723 edition!) of Anderson's *Constitutions*—the version that is sometimes described as 'regressive' compared to the first.[88]

As for the presumed propaganda by certain elements of English Masonry for 'religious dogmatism' and their supposedly 'spiritualist' obsessions, we only need to read the words of its deputy Grand Master in 2011 (the number three of the United Grand Lodge of England) to get an idea of it:

> We need to be absolutely clear when we discuss our pure ancient masonry that we belong to a secular organisation, that is to say a non-religious organisation ... Freemasonry itself, as we all know, is neither a substitute for nor an alternative to religion. It certainly does not deal in spirituality—it does not have any sacraments.

---

[88] In the *Dedication*, on page v. 1738 version?.

... The Craft sought to encourage men to be loyal to their country, to obey the law, to try to be better behaved, to consider their relations with others and to make themselves more extensively serviceable to their fellow men—that is to say their wider communities. In other words, to pursue a moral life.[89]

Who in France would not sign up to such a program forbidding all 'religious' spirituality as foreign to the field of Freemasonry? Who would object to this affirmation of secularity?

That said, we are talking about England, where nothing is simple. Jonathan Spence immediately added,

It is, however, a secular organisation that is supportive of religion: it is an absolute requirement for all our members to believe in a supreme being.

'Secular' yet 'religious': such is the nature of English Freemasonry. One might say of the English Freemason, as Montesquieu's characters say of Usbek in *Persian Letters*, 'How can one be 'English' [or 'Persian']?'

Nonetheless, many French Freemasons who are passionate about Masonry (and even the others) maintain a sort of persistent fascination with this world of British Masonry. Since it appears inaccessible and filled with ineradicable prejudices, we find ourselves thinking that we can skew things, play games: in a word, 'play the Frenchman'!

With the Call of Basel, some thought the French were 'breaching the English defences', arguing that it was possible to be recognised and therefore regular by the grace

---

[89] Jonathan Spence—Deputy Grand Master's speech, September 14, 2011 (UGLE website).

of the five Grand Lodges, and that London would either give in or lose face before the rebellion.

This was a serious misunderstanding of the global regular landscape and how it worked: the outcome leaves no doubt about this. Of course, as we have seen, the regular Masonic world is not uniform, but we should not exaggerate: nothing lasting can be achieved without consent from London and at least the benevolent neutrality of the Americans.

In the eyes of the English, only recognition from London constitutes 'true' regularity, and this is generally the result of a long process. However, on this point, the UGLE has so far never allowed its principles to be compromised in the slightest. Consequently, as displeasing as this may be for those who want to create confusion and who mistake their wishes for reality, I would like to restate this obvious fact: there is no regularity (in the Anglo-Saxon sense of the word, which is the only one everyone is interested in) without explicit recognition from London!

And let me reiterate clearly that to obtain it, a price (an entirely honorable one) must be paid.

Although this has already been stated above, it is necessary to emphasise that almost all cases of 'de-recognition' have been connected with a Grand Lodge not respecting the clause about belief in a Supreme Being. We should not be fooled by speculation about the supposed differences between the 1929 version of the *Basic Principles* and the 'modern' 1989 version:[90] the latter was a project that was never adopted and that features nowhere in the current official documents of the UGLE, and particularly not in its *Book of Constitutions*! The recent declarations of the

---

[90] Which, moreover, did not change much.

Deputy Grand Master, mentioned above, leave no room for doubt:

> It is an absolute requirement for all our members to believe in a supreme being.

This is an essential fact of Anglo-Saxon culture, according to which (even if the situation obviously changes over time) religious adherence is a constituent of social identity. English doctrine has therefore not changed, and it will not change anytime soon. As for the supposedly 'American martingale', we have seen what was to be thought of this.

Of course, the culture of an old 'post-Catholic' country like France makes this question a hot topic. France is a country where, according to the most recent opinion surveys, 25–30% of people at the very most say they believe in God. This is compared to at least 60% in England and over 80% in the United States. However, beyond this decisive context, it is the very relationship to religion and to faith that has become problematic in France. Today, many people most commonly think of religion as a blind obedience to an intolerant Church that dominates minds. This is particularly the case among those who abandoned any religious tradition long ago. It is again worth emphasising here that Masonry, born in a Protestant country, is for the most part regular in Protestant countries, and mostly 'liberal' in currently or formerly Catholic countries.

Much has also been said about the ban on inter-visiting with irregular Obediences—that is, Obediences that are not recognised (since, it goes without saying, the British treat the oddity of a 'regular and unrecognised' Obedience exactly as they would treat an irregular Obedience). Unfortunately, once again, some people believed that trickery would work. True, lying about the *Great* Architect of the Universe (to oneself or to others) is a possibility, but it is harder to cheat with inter-visiting. The abundant vocabulary of certain French Masonic leaders in the period between 2012 and 2014 provides a sad illustration of this. It is regrettable that in this affair—which has been the talk of the French Masonic world since 2012, which created much disorder, but which came to its expected end—the French pretended to believe that this rule had become obsolete and that there could be 'compromises with Heaven'. This was not the case. The regular Grand Lodges clearly reiterated this to anyone who would listen. But for those who played deaf ...

The question is more whether the Anglo-Saxons will eventually come to understand that what goes for them and in their country must be adapted to harmonise with a continental European culture that differs significantly from theirs, and whether, when they have understood this, they will care.

Maybe one day, the UGLE—and also the American Grand Lodges—will change its point of view and its practices. However, this will only happen if it is in its interest to do so, and certainly not under pressure. Admittedly, the UGLE does not exercise the same global influence it did before, and it is well aware of this,[91] but its 'network' remains considerable, and no credible challenger has emerged yet.

It is worth mentioning here a fact that is pleasing in this context. On March 10, 1999, the UGLE officially published the following declaration:

---

[91] Already, in November 2007, its Pro Grand Master at the time, Lord Northampton, claimed that it no longer wanted to be 'the Masonic policeman of the world.'

There exist in England and Wales at least two Grand Lodges solely for women. Except that these bodies admit women, they are, so far as can be ascertained,[92] otherwise *regular in their practice*. There is also one which admits both men and women to membership.[93] They are not recognised by this Grand Lodge and inter-visitation may not take place. There are, however, discussions from time to time with the women's Grand Lodges on matters of mutual concern. Brethren [of the UGLE] are therefore free to explain to non-Masons, if asked, that Freemasonry is not confined to men (even though this Grand Lodge does not itself admit women).

Therefore, we should not be too quick to judge, but we should ourselves seek to understand and take into account elements that are not necessarily part of our own culture. We should try to leave behind convenient posi-

---

[92] This is an extremely interesting passage. It shows that in order to be certain, it is necessary to have gone and seen what is forbidden! In its internal documents, to justify the eviction of women, the UGLE evokes only the masculine traditions of the ancient 'Stone Masons'. Nevertheless, we should note that *The Order of Women Freemasons*, which has around six thousand members who call themselves 'Brethren', is a carbon copy of the UGLE in terms of decorations, degrees, rituals, and landmarks! It celebrated its hundred-year anniversary in great ceremony in 2008 at the Royal Albert Hall, and it maintains no relationship with the 'liberal' women's Grand Lodges on the Continent.

[93] This refers to the British Federation of the Droit Humain, whose website reminds readers that it 'recognizes the existence of a Creating Principle, which some call the Supreme Being, and which many Freemasons refer to as the Great Architect of the Universe'.. A split in 2001 created the Grand Lodge of Freemasonry for Men and Women, which presents 'a belief in a Supreme Being' and the presence of the 'V.S.L. writings of the great religions' as 'an essential requirement'.

tions in favour of an open and tolerant approach. This can be achieved in particular via better knowledge of the past of various parties.

European Freemasonry is the product of a complex and turbulent history and has taken on several faces in almost three centuries. However, all of these are derived from a common source, in which we can recognise ourselves or from which we can distance ourselves. However, under no circumstances can we ignore it, if we wish to fully understand an institution that is sometimes as mysterious for its members as it is in the eyes of the general public.

At a turning point in its history marked by a glorious past, and today facing a certain decline, in both England and the United States, English and above all American Freemasonry is considering its future and taking the opportunity to re-examine its foundations, as well as perhaps some of its practices. If more French Freemasons were to abandon some of their certainties and take a step along the same path, what is sometimes seen as a divisive conflict for global Masonry might start to be seen for what it really is: a misunderstanding that could undoubtedly be smoothed out by means of a new intellectual 'Channel tunnel'.

CHAPTER 9
The Heart of the Problem

A fter this long but necessary historical overview, are
we any clearer in our understanding of a notion that
some exploit at their leisure—or shamelessly distort?

The results of this step-by-step investigation could objec-
tively lead us to admit (whether we like it or not) that
the following points are facts of history, and to accept the
reasonable consequences of them:

1. 'Regularity', a notion introduced into Masonic
vocabulary by the English and very quickly tak-
en up by the French in the eighteenth century,
initially simply referred (according to the natural meaning of this word) to conformity with
the administrative obligations of a Brother and
his Lodge towards a Grand Lodge whose authority they recognised. In return, the Grand
Lodge gave them the rights to benefit from its
mutual assistance work.

2. At the end of the nineteenth century, having
become the only Masonic power in the world's
leading empire, with Lodges all around the
globe, in reaction to the decision of the 1877
Convent of the Grand Orient de France (and
undoubtedly because of the historical importance of French Masonry), the UGLE judged it
necessary to specify that in its eyes, since time
immemorial, the first of all the landmarks (a
term that was and is still extremely vague) had

ROGER DACHEZ

always been and remained the belief in God.
The main parallel of this, specified later, was
that the Masonic oath had to be sworn on the
Volume of Sacred Law, representing the 'revelation from above'. This volume gave the said oath
'a sacred character'.

3. For the first time, in 1913, the UGLE gave a
label to a Grand Lodge in France, 'recognising'
the Grande Loge nationale indépendante et
régulière (subsequently the GLNF). Masonry
that was 'recognised' by London commonly
came to be called 'regular masonry'.

4. Forced to make its doctrine more specific, in the
face of the expected appearance of numerous
independent Grand Lodges both in the British
Empire and in the rest of the world, the UGLE,
followed by the Home Grand Lodges (Scotland and Ireland), set down this doctrine as a
whole for the first time in the 1929 *Basic Principles*. There was nothing revolutionary about
these, and they confirmed old convictions. All
the comments made about them by the English
Masonic authorities since then emphasise that,
out of the eight points listed, the most important by far are points 2, 3 and 6. These relate to
the belief in a Supreme Being and to the Volume of Sacred Law. Decisions to 'derecognise' a
Grand Lodge that was formerly considered regular were almost always based on a failure to respect these principles. In 1952, the Information
Commission on Recognition of the Conference
of Grand Masters in North America only stipulated three Standards of Recognition, the most

significant of which was 'belief in God'.

5. This doctrine would be solemnly reiterated in a text that was finally published in 1949 but devised from 1938: the *Aims and Relationships of the Craft*. This committed the three Home Grand Lodges and basically repeated the content of the Basic Principles.

6. Since the end of the war, many Grand Lodges around the world have decided to officially submit to this doctrine, in order to obtain recognition from London. They make up what is usually called 'regular Masonry'.

7. Although it is perfectly clear that 'recognition' is not 'regularity', it is just as certain that, in Anglo-Saxon practice, a 'regular' Grand Lodge (or one presumed to be regular!) that is not yet recognised is treated in exactly the same way as a Grand Lodge that is considered to be irregular. In particular, no inter-visiting with such a Lodge is permitted. The failure to respect this clause is in fact the second most frequent motive for the suspension or breaking off of relations between London and a hitherto recognised Lodge.

8. 'Regular Masonry', with no other comment, therefore signifies by omission and by default 'regular Masonry according to the Anglo-Saxon standards'. In the international Masonic community, it is always understood in this way, and it is never necessary to specify 'regular Masonry according to x or y', since this distinction is meaningless and has no place in current practice.

9. It seems reasonable to consider the fact that this definition of regularity is shared or claimed by about 90% of Masonry in the world. Although the community of 'regular' Grand Lodges is not homogeneous (some of them do not recognise each other or are not even recognised by London), this is never because some of them question the *Basic Principles*, but because of other considerations. These include the viability of a Grand Lodge, its age, its representativeness, its internal administration, and local disputes, among other things.

10. It is therefore equally reasonable to think that we should not 'play' with the word 'regular' by declaring that all Grand Lodges that decide they want to be regular are (a habit that is particularly widespread in France).

11. This amounts to saying that we should not essentialise the word 'regularity' by making it a generic synonym for 'good Masonry', 'true Masonry' or 'serious Masonry', when the content attributed to it from one Obedience to the next is sometimes very different. It seems that everywhere in the world apart from France, 'regularity' simply means 'conformity with the 1929 *Basic Principles*'.

12. This careless (and often provocative) usage of the word 'regularity' has two consequences. Firstly, it robs it of any precise meaning. Secondly and above all, it maintains deliberate ambiguity in the discourses of certain Masonic circles, implying that a Grand Lodge might well be recognised by London, even though it is not,

and that it has the right, in a way, from that moment and on its own initiative, to claim the 'label' of regularity that it has in fact been refused by the global 'regular' community.

13. At the end of the day, it would be more appropriate, honest, rigorous and favourable to a tranquil climate if Grand Lodges in France that are not recognised by London were to describe their Masonry, if they wish, according to the spirit it gives them: 'traditional', 'spiritual' (or 'spiritualist'), 'initiatory' (!), or even 'humanist', 'liberal', 'adogmatic', 'secular' and so forth. Similarly, it would be desirable for certain sections of the Masonic community to stop calling others 'irregular'.

If there is one moral demand that applies to everyone in Masonry, it is undoubtedly the demand to be 'true.' By this, I mean recognising without artifice what one is or is not, what one does or does not think and what one believes or refuses to believe, without red herrings, ulterior motives, or mental reservations. It even seems that we have all vowed to do this.

I wish to emphasise once again that if we consent to stop beating around the bush and playing sly tricks, to stop these little strategies of Masonic policy or flattering the ego of supposed experts who have become prophets, being 'regular' simply means unambiguously sharing the points listed in the Basic Principles, according to the unequivocal interpretation given to the most significant of them. Regularity is not a value in itself. It does not ennoble those who claim it. It is only a descriptive and technical term that refers to a certain position and therefore has an immediate consequence: the possibility of being recognised by London and its friends, and joining the largest Masonic community in the world.

But France, whose Masonic history is as complicated as its political and institutional history, has invented a complex Masonry with (to use an architectural metaphor) variable geometry. We can celebrate or lament this, but we cannot deny it. In France, we have therefore imported and dramatised a conflict that should never have existed.

The gulf that some people today place between regular[94] Masonry (pure and untainted, entirely initiatory, traditional and spiritual) and so-called 'societal' Masonry is a crude approximation of the truth of French Masonry, which is much more subtle and nuanced.

In France, on the philosophical and religious level, and also on the level of 'genre', there is a thousand-colored spectrum of Masonry. Some Masons (around twenty-five thousand) have made choices that allow them to fraternise in Lodges and correspond with 90% of Masons in the world. This is a coherent and respectable decision. Others have made a different choice, opting to speak to and work above all with French Masons, rather than with Masons around the world. Nevertheless, between these two extremes, there are multiple nuances and many points of contention: mixed lodges, the place of societal debate, the importance or otherwise of religious beliefs, and so forth. We should add to this a question that does not arise in England or the United States but that plays a major role in France: that of the Rite.[95] Consequently,

---

[94] Including when this word refers to a Masonry that is not recognized.

[95] All British Masons practice the 'Ritual of the Union' in blue Lodges. In France, this ritual is represented by what is known as the 'Rite

there are certainly many more than 'three paths' (as a lamentable and highly interest-driven schematic representation would have us believe). Each of the Obediences in the French Masonic landscape, from the smallest to largest, has found a name and a place for itself.

However, despite this apparent disorder, which the great Obediences often become annoyed about without always analysing the underlying causes for it,[96] everything could be simple. Masonry could look like a family whose members, despite their differences and even their small disputes, all respect their constraints and apply all of the principles that they proclaim (fraternal generosity, true tolerance and so forth) if personal ambitions and the egotism of Obediences did not all too often call the shots.

Just for once, I would like to cite Oswald Wirth, mentioned above. As I said, I do not share his interpretation of the 'schism' between the French and the British in the Masonic domain, but I wholeheartedly agree with the plea that he wrote on this matter. It is Wirth at his best:

> So let us not seek Masonic unity anywhere but in ourselves. It will not come from any convent decision or from an agreement between Masonic governments: true unity can only be made in our hearts and minds.
>
> It is made in the hearts of all those who feel themselves to be Freemasons, whatever their

---

Emulation', with countless but minimal variants. In no way does this stop them practicing an impressive number of high degrees, including those of the Ancient and Accepted Scottish Rite, which for them begins only at the eighteenth degree and has no influence in symbolic Lodges.

[96] See our observations concerning this in Barat, Bauer, and Dachez, *Les Promesses de l'aube* (2013).

Obedience; all that remains is to make it effective in our minds, which are still not enlightened enough. All the efforts of the friends of unity must go into spreading enlightenment, because we can only be united in work, and to work together as one, a clear understanding is vital.[97]

So how do we 'spread enlightenment' rather than obscurity and confusion? How do we move beyond our postures, to avoid imposture?

Perhaps, as Francis Drake recommended in his famous speech in 1726, this can be done by cultivating the 'three great principles' of Freemasonry: 'brotherly love, relief and truth'. Or, as the old French Masonic catechisms assert, by coming to the Lodge to 'submit your will, subdue your passions'. That would be a good start!

However, it is also to be achieved by allowing sincerity, goodwill, honest work, study and kindness to others to prevail. These are human qualities before they are Masonic ones. We need to act against the liars and the fakers, the ambitious and the arrogant, if Masonry does not wish to end up looking like a caricature—and if it wants to finally live as it believes it should speak.

---

[97] Oswald Wirth, 'Notre unité spirituelle', in *Qui est régulier?*, 114.

APPENDICES

Basic Principles for Grand Lodge Recognition (UGLE, 1929)[98]

The M.W. The Grand Master having expressed a desire that the Board (of general affairs)[99] would draw up a statement of the Basic Principles on which this Grand Lodge could be invited to recognise any Grand Lodge applying for recognition by the English Jurisdiction, the Board of General Purposes has gladly complied. The result, as follows, has been approved by the Grand Master and it will form the basis of a questionnaire to be forwarded in future to each Jurisdiction requesting English recognition. The Board desires that not only such bodies but also the Brethren generally throughout the Grand Master's Jurisdiction shall be fully informed as to those Basic Principles of Freemasonry for which the Grand Lodge of England has stood throughout its history.

1. Regularity of origin; i.e. each Grand Lodge shall have been established lawfully by a duly recognised Grand Lodge or by three or more regularly constituted Lodges.

---

[98] Sometimes in France, reference is made to a more recent version from 1986, which slightly simplified the 1929 version—without altering it perceptibly. In any case, it was only a project proposed by the Board of General Purposes, and was never adopted by the Grand Lodge. Consequently, the official texts of the UGLE still only mention the 1929 version—the only authoritative version in its eyes. It is therefore pointless to comment on this matter.

[99] The structure (partly elected and partly nominated by the Grand Master) that is in charge of the general administration of the UGLE.

2. That a belief in the G.A.O.T.U. and His revealed will shall be an essential qualification for membership.

3. That all Initiates shall take their Obligation on or in full view of the open Volume of the Sacred Law, by which is meant the revelation from above which is binding on the conscience of the particular individual who is being initiated.

4. That the membership of the Grand Lodge and individual Lodges shall be composed exclusively of men; and that each Grand Lodge shall have no Masonic intercourse of any kind with mixed Lodges or bodies which admit women to membership.

5. That the Grand Lodge shall have sovereign jurisdiction over the Lodges under its control; i.e. that it shall be a responsible, independent, self-governing organisation, with sole and undisputed authority over the Craft or Symbolic Degrees (Entered Apprentice, Fellow Craft, and Master Mason) within its Jurisdiction; and shall not in any way be subject to, or divide such authority with, a Supreme Council or other Power claiming any control or supervision over those degrees.

6. That the three Great Lights of Freemasonry (namely, the Volume of the Sacred Law, the Square, and the Compasses) shall always be exhibited when the Grand Lodge or its subordinate Lodges are at work, the chief of these being the Volume of the Sacred Law.[100]

---

[100] Let us emphasize here that the Three Great Lights are a rather minor point (point 6 of 8 in total), particularly the Compasses and

7. That the discussion of religion and politics within the Lodge shall be strictly prohibited.

8. That the principles of the Antient Landmarks, customs and usages of the Craft shall be strictly observed.

Aims and Relationships of the Craft[101] (Home Grand Lodges, 1949)

1. From time to time the United Grand Lodge of England has deemed it desirable to set forth in precise form the aims of Freemasonry as consistently practised under its Jurisdiction since it came into being as an organised body in 1717, and also to define the principles governing its relations with those other Grand Lodges with which it is in fraternal accord.

2. In view of representations which have been received, and of statements recently issued which have distorted or obscured the true objects of Freemasonry, it is once again considered necessary to emphasise certain fundamental principles of the Order

3. The first condition of admission into and mem-

---

the Square, which are 'only' symbols. This cannot be said of the Volume of Sacred Law, presented here as the 'chief of these' but already consecrated by point 3 of the *Basic Principles* as evoking 'the revelation from above' and as 'binding on the conscience' of the initiate, which means that it is not just a symbol in the English version.

[101] 'Craft' evidently refers to the three operative terms of Apprentice, Companion, and Master, and in British Masonry it designates Masonry of the first three degrees, under the exclusive regime of a Grand Lodge, independent of the high degrees.

bership of, the Order is a belief in the Supreme Being. This is essential and admits of no compromise.

4. The Bible, referred to by Freemasons as the Volume of the Sacred Law, is always open in the Lodges. Every Candidate is required to take his Obligation on that book or on the Volume which is held by his particular creed to impart sanctity to an oath or promise taken upon it.

5. Everyone who enters Freemasonry is, at the outset, strictly forbidden to countenance any act which may have a tendency to subvert the peace and good order of society; he must pay due obedience to the law of any state in which he resides or which may afford him protection, and he must never be remiss in the allegiance due to the Sovereign of his native land.

6. While English Freemasonry thus inculcates in each of its members the duties of loyalty and citizenship, it reserves to the individual the right to hold his own opinion with regard to public affairs. But neither in any Lodge, nor at any time in his capacity as a Freemason, is he permitted to discuss or to advance his views on theological or political questions.

7. The Grand Lodge has always consistently refused to express any opinion on questions of foreign or domestic state policy either at home or abroad, and it will not allow its name to be associated with any action; however humanitarian it may appear to be, which infringes its unalterable policy of standing aloof from every

question affecting the relations between one government and another, or between political parties, or questions as to rival theories of government.

8. The Grand Lodge is aware that there do exist Bodies, styling themselves Freemasons, which do not adhere to these principles, and while that attitude exists the Grand Lodge of England refuses absolutely to have any relations with such Bodies or to regard them as Freemasons.

9. The Grand Lodge of England is a Sovereign and independent Body practising Freemasonry only within the three Degrees and only within the limits defined in its Constitution as 'pure Antient Masonry.' It does not recognise or admit the existence of any superior Masonic authority, however styled.

10. On more than one occasion the Grand Lodge has refused, and will continue to refuse, to participate in Conferences with so-called International Associations claiming to represent Freemasonry, which admit to membership Bodies failing to conform strictly to the principles upon which the Grand Lodge of England is founded. The Grand Lodge does not admit any such claim, nor can its views be represented by any such Association.

11. There is no secret with regard to any of the basic principles of Freemasonry, some of which have been stated above. The Grand Lodge will always consider the recognition of those Grand Lodges which profess and practise and can show that

they have consistently professed and practised, those established and unaltered principles, but in no circumstances will it enter into discussion with a view to any new or varied interpretation of them. They must be accepted and practised wholeheartedly and in their entirety by those who desire to be recognised as Freemasons by the United Grand Lodge of England.

Standards for Recognition (USA, 1952)

Since the delegates of this Conference change each year, it important to restate the Standards of Recognition adopted for our guidance when this Commission [on Information for recognition] was formed in 1952. These are the guidelines used to evaluate Regularity of a Grand Lodge, and thereby determine whether it is worthy of consideration for Recognition by our member Grand Lodges [of the Conference].

This Commission provides this data for use by our Grand Lodges, and does not attempt to influence or recommend what action should be taken. The Commission serves in an investigative and advisory capacity only.

The Standards of Recognition are summarised as follows:

1. Legitimacy of Origin.
2. Exclusive Territorial Jurisdiction, except by mutual consent and/or treaty.[102]

---

[102] This clearly means that no Lodge under a new authority can be created in a territory where there is already a Grand Lodge. This has always been a sensitive subject in a federal structure like the United States, where the principle of exclusive territorial jurisdiction was born. We can observe that it does not feature in the *Basic Principles*.

3. Adherence to the Ancient Landmarks—specifically, a Belief in God, the Volume of Sacred Law as an indispensable part of the Furniture of the Lodge,[103] and the prohibition of the discussion of politics and religion.

---

[103] Because, in typically Anglo-Saxon and Protestant logic, it is a sign of God's revealed will and makes the vow on this book sacred. This is explicitly repeated in the two other texts mentioned in these appendices.

www.ingramcontent.com/pod-product-compliance
Lightning Source LLC
Chambersburg PA
CBHW060507280326
41933CB00014B/2886